TALES FROM AN OLD SOLDIER'S FOOTLOCKER

TALES FROM AN OLD SOLDIER'S FOOTLOCKER

STORIES WRITTEN ON SLEEPLESS NIGHTS BY
A SAILOR, SOLDIER, AG ADVISOR, MILITARY
INTELLIGENCE AGENT, SENIOR FOREIGN FIELD
ADVISOR, TEACHER, ARMY RANGER

LOGAN BARBEE

TALES FROM AN OLD SOLDIER'S FOOTLOCKER
STORIES WRITTEN ON SLEEPLESS NIGHTS BY A SAILOR, SOLDIER, AG ADVISOR, MILITARY INTELLIGENCE AGENT, SENIOR FOREIGN FIELD ADVISOR, TEACHER, ARMY RANGER. LOGAN BARBEE

iUniverse books may be ordered through booksellers or by contacting:

iUniverse
1663 Liberty Drive
Bloomington, IN 47403
www.iuniverse.com
844-349-9409

ISBN: 978-1-6632-4420-8 (sc)
ISBN: 978-1-6632-4421-5 (hc)
ISBN: 978-1-6632-4419-2 (e)

Library of Congress Control Number: 2022919600

Print information available on the last page.

iUniverse rev. date: 01/17/2024

These stories were written for my children—Matthew, Brandon, Jim, and Morgan. When I'm gone, you'll be able to learn a little more about me. These words might help explain what you see in yourselves. Thank you for all you have brought into my life.

CONTENTS

Introduction...ix

What I've Been Up to Lately.......................................1
A Little about Me 2
How I Overcame Having a Small Brain 5
A Call I'll Always Remember 8
I'm a Sure Bet for Political Correctness Hell............11
A Young Merchant Marine Sailor.............................13
FFA and the American Flag 18
Lightered Wood Provides a Blessing in Many, Many Ways.........21
Lonely Nights in Foreign Lands...............................23
Out of the Mouth of a Six-Year-Old 25
Rode My First Two Bulls at Fifty Years Old...........26
Thankful for Dogwood Trees 31
The Gift..33
Fourteen-Year-Olds versus the US Navy SEALs 35
Where Is the Fruit? 40
If I Were Giving Advice to Myself............................52
Tinker, Sailor, Soldier, Educator, County Agent, Special
Agent, Spy...53
A Profile of Duty, Honor, and Country: The Danny Hassig
Story 62
Grandmother Nellie, Uncle Willie, and Family Influences
on My Early Life 69
How I Remember My Dad 73

Remembering Brandon 78
Remembering Jimmy Clyde Sexton: Friend, Cousin, Good
Buddy—Killed in Action, Vietnam 82
The Engagement in Which Jimmy Was Killed 84
The Doctor I Called Slow Leak 86
The Christmas Party 87
A Collector of Characters 91
The Map and the Making of an Intelligence Operator 93
The Joke 96
How Do I Explain That Feeling? 98
How Can You Explain That Feeling? 99
Flinthead Arrows 102
Spear Hunting: The Modern-Day Spear Hunter 103
Ambushed 112
Gators in the River 114
I Didn't Know What an Army Ranger Was 116
Just Another Day in Iraq 121
My Hog Went to Iraq and Back 124
Rambling Thoughts of Gratitude 132
SSPP: Supersecret Pigeon Project 135
The First Annual Bosnia International Invitational
Longbow Championship 138
Weapons to the Ministry 143
God Was in Iraq 147
Last Rocket and Mortar Attack 150

Introduction

In basic training, every soldier used to keep a wooden footlocker at the head or foot of the bed. It was a place to store trinkets, memorabilia, photos, and keepsakes. That's how I think about this book—a place to hold this hodgepodge of stories, the remembrances of a former teacher, merchant seaman, army officer, field advisor, and dad.

It will be up to the reader to determine which version of myself wrote each story. That's what happens on sleepless nights—tales are remembered that had been stored away in my old army footlocker. Each item brings back memories and stories that need to be shared so that my children might have a little insight into their dad's identity, personality, and legacy.

These are just a few of those stories, written on sleepless nights by a sailor, soldier, AG advisor, military intelligence agent, senior foreign field advisor, teacher, and Army Ranger.

WHAT I'VE BEEN UP TO LATELY

I AM IN THE PROCESS OF FINISHING THREE BOOKS I STARTED many years ago and writing two others at the same time. My ADD (attention deficit disorder) should help explain some of the reasons why I do certain things a certain way. Yes, I know that's not usually the way writing goes for most authors. But my poor spelling, my grammar, and my ADD have gotten me this far. Let's see where they take me from here on out.

I'll be pushing out some stories through social media as well. I have over fifty stories outlined—some partially written, some drafted, and others with only titles. I'm weak and often come up short. I can take criticism with a little sprinkling of encouragement. I wrote this book so my kids will have a keepsake of their old man's exploits. We all have our worries, thoughts, needs, loves, and dislikes. We only go through this world once, so I understand. Maybe these books will help answer my children's and grandchildren's questions.

To my friends and family: I hope I didn't embarrass you too much. I've been told I write similarly to how I speak. I'm just being myself.

To my readers: please understand I'm trying to keep it folksy.

And to my teachers: I was a poor student. Don't blame yourselves.

A Little about Me

When I was a kid, I worked part-time after school, and on weekends with my uncle Wade Monroe Smith at the Pure Oil full-service filling station in a little river town named after an old Native American chief, Blount. I was raised in the country, along Graves Creek, in Calhoun County, North Florida, and I grew up with great cousins and good friends: the Sexton boys—Jerry Shields, Wayne Redd, and Marlon Lewis—and a few Black friends—Clifford, Quaky, and Eljay. I lived with my wonderful grandmother, uncles, mother, and father, along with my younger brother, Salari. I enjoyed a great country upbringing.

My first traumatic experience occurred when I was thirteen, and we moved from the country to the town, something I would never wish on anyone. I loved the country living. That move resulted in me becoming a C student—I was previously an A student. With some guidance from my newfound friends, I transitioned from a naive innocent to a street outlaw. I learned just how much I didn't know by hanging out with Ivey Bailey, Bill Reeder, Tommy Kent, Wyman McCormack, Wayne Couch, and other street runners and performers. Most lived two different lives: they had a public personality and an underground street persona. Some hid it better than others. I struggled to adapt and keep up with them. Those experiences served me well in several of my adult careers, including my tenure as a counterintelligence officer and my work in agency politics and missions around the world.

I was an actor, and the world was my stage.

Another significant event that helped me to consider what I was going to do with my life was working with my uncle changing log-truck tires, which are called split-rim tires. One Saturday, after I had helped Uncle Wade change and air up over thirty split-rims, I decided after that last boom of rim and tire seating into place that I wasn't going to do this much longer.

1. So the first two transitional activities in my early life worked to my benefit later. I was moving away from all the things I loved in life—country living, with confidence in myself and others—to a place that showed me how to be two-faced, critical, cynical, and corrupt. I fought the temptation, but not very well. The second early event was airing up over thirty split-rim tires on a long hot Saturday, when my time could have been better spent at the creek.

2. I hope I haven't misled anyone so far. There were many good things and people that came out of my transition into a halfway townie. I had many positive friends and influences. Rob Parrish and I were friends in both town and county. There was George Ed Smith, Tommy Kent, the Tillmans, and even some of the ones who taught me the other side of things. There were also the good sides. I was never convicted or sentenced to prison, and all these events contributed to a very pleasing and never dull childhood.

After graduating high school in 1967, I enrolled at Chipola College. Feeling like a draft dodger, Chipola was packed with students. I then enlisted in the merchant marines in 1968 with my good friend Jerry Hatcher. Vietnam was an escalating conflict and had considerable influence on many people's decisions at that time.

In 1969, being drafted into the US Army was a part of growing up for many of my friends and classmates.

Transitioning back into society and pursuing a more serious educational endeavor was next after my military service. The GI Bill, most of the time two or three jobs, and a full-time class schedule weren't too much for a young Army Ranger back then. I grew in boundless ways, with no challenge too great.

I enjoyed six years of teaching. The kids taught me how to teach. I certainly learned more from them than they did from me. Teaching agricultural classes and FFA was a wonderful time. They were great kids, and they learned many life lessons while creating new opportunities for themselves. Many times I wished I had stayed with teaching. It was a magical time, and I could see their growth and their bright futures. I just hope I never, ever let them down.

The University of Florida, the US Army Reserves, and many active deployments awaited me over the next twenty-five years. I enjoyed and grew with the times. It was also a special time for gaining new stories. There have been so many special folks, civilian and military, who have entered my life. I want to tell readers about them.

I lost a son, and my life changed.

Back to Iraq and many years of stories to tell. I was the same, but different. Military, US State Department, contractor—I had to get back to real life. My old life was dead; it died with Brandon. But I have three very precious children: Jim, Matthew, and Morgan; Bonita, my other half; and two stepsons, Justin and Chris. Life is returning, and I hope I'm worthy.

How I Overcame Having
a Small Brain

A FEW THINGS I LEARNED GROWING UP: THE LITTLE BITS OF knowledge that I put to muscle memory became my normal actions.

We remember, some folks say, only about 10 percent from what we hear, 40 percent from what we watch, and upward of 90 percent by what we do. I am not sure about the percentages, but the spread seems right. The best lesson to come from this is to learn from doing and then keep it up.

I found out that watching other people can help strengthen one's knowledge base as well as your financial stability. Let them make the mistakes and then learn from their mistakes.

From my seat at the back of the classroom, I looked at my buddies and realized something: if I sit in the back of the classroom, I must have a little brain. My friends and I all had mediocre grades ranging from B's to C's and sometimes D's. As I looked toward the front of the class, I found out where the As sat.

After moving from the country to a small town at the youthful age of thirteen, I regressed from earning A's to becoming an average C student who formed some bad habits. It took many years of fumbling around without goals or plans for me to realize something: I needed direction. But with my little brain, how was I going to make up for lost time?

I couldn't make my brain grow any larger, so what could I do?

After all, I wanted to be able to provide for a family in the future, and my limited brain capacity was going to hold me back if I didn't change course.

Looking back, I see what I did to overcome my little brain problem. I was raised with manners, so I used them. It doesn't take a big brain to have good manners nor does it take a large brain to arrive a little early and stay a little later to get things done.

I was starting to understand something: anyone can succeed, even with a little brain, but it might take a little more perspiration.

I became aware of a few things that would help me, or anyone else, move ahead in life and make up for lost learning and study time. No big brain needed to be honest, have integrity, be of good character, be loyal, be enthusiastic, develop a solid work ethic, demonstrate social skills, and, of course, use manners.

These acquired attributes and a positive attitude, fueled and fertilized a growth that helped me conclude that my little brain reform movement could and would help me accomplish a few goals that I set for myself, which would lead to the future family I hoped to have one day. During this process, I had been watching other folks who seemed to be on top of things. I watched positive people, people who carried themselves straight and upright. These positive people were happy and content in life.

As I considered the roads I needed to travel to reach my destination, I realized each road had plenty of doors, gates, and ways of passing. Which road would help me be the person Mama would like me to be? Which road would not embarrass my family? And which road would help me provide a comfortable lifestyle for my own family?

Always keep in mind that the road we travel will be uniquely ours. No two roads are the same. We are all faced with choices in life. Of course, we can always blame being poor, a lack of opportunities, our shortcomings, social status, birth privileges, skin color, poor luck, or our parents. But blaming everything and everyone else will never pay the piper.

A retired senior army sergeant recently expressed his gratitude to several mentors and exemplars he had in his life. I'm sure some of those mentors helped to show him the way and offered good advice.

Many set good examples, I'm sure, but some might have set bad examples from which we can also learn. Anytime we can learn from others' mistakes rather than our own, it's much cheaper! And it also shortens the learning curve.

Years later, when in college—Chipola, FAMU, FSU, and UWF—I used a little trick I learned years earlier. Growing up, I realized all people are prejudiced in some way. We don't mean to be, but we are, even teachers. I used this little trick, as I call it, at the start of any new classes. I would move up to the front of the classroom, usually the second seat from the front on the right side of the classroom. I wasn't sure if I was fooling myself or the instructors, but there I sat, all smiles. In doing so, I persuaded the instructor into thinking I was one of the smart ones. It worked, and to this day I believe I received better grades as a result of that smart move.

And on top of that, I usually earned another higher letter grade because I was away from my peers and more attentive.

It's said by some that we only use about 10 percent of our brain capacity anyway. I believe that.

A Call I'll Always Remember

O N A SUNDAY AFTERNOON I RECEIVED A CALL OUT OF THE blue, a call anyone would love to receive. A soldier from my past called me and said while he and his family were sitting in church he had glanced down while opening his Bible, and there it was—my name, which he had inscribed next to a passage. He said he just had to call me.

Who wouldn't want their name written in the Bible?

He went on to say that one day in Iraq he was downtrodden and feeling pretty low and about ready to call it quits. Continuing, he said, "And then you must have had an indication that something was wrong, as you came hurriedly up to me, put your arm around my shoulder, and asked, 'What's going on?'"

I only vaguely knew this young soldier, but I had been paying attention. What little I knew of this young man I had picked up from other soldiers, in briefings, and by watching his interactions with his peers. I knew from his language and how he talked he was a loyal family man, deeply religious, and very patriotic.

I believe he was an engineer by trade, and he brought those skills to a dangerous country to try to help out when he didn't have to. I knew he and his team went out into the red zone more often than many of his comrades and that he "sorta" worked for the commander.

That day, in that parking lot, as he was walking, I knew something wasn't right. He had those drooping shoulders. He was carrying a heavy load—a burden.

I didn't remember those events until he reminded me of the situation and what I said.

I've asked, *What's going on?* to myself and many others throughout the years. Maybe not the same words, but some kind word or gesture can often make a difference in someone's life. But this time it brought him back on course. I know that day made a difference.

Well, he will never know what that call to me several years ago meant, unless he reads this little story. His call was much appreciated and made me reflect on things in my life. One never knows how the little things we do might affect others.

This soldier was a subordinate to me, a young guy, and not in my immediate chain of command. But he was one of our soldiers and one I had admired from afar. He had never been out on a mission with me. We had not had much interaction, but I felt like I knew him. He was very loyal to his family, whom he loved and missed dearly. He had strong religious beliefs and was a hardworking, dedicated soldier. Those are traits anyone can admire.

I very much loved our soldiers, especially ones who cared and gave so much of themselves. I also loved the ones who had not yet found themselves.

"Colonel," the caller said, "I just had to call today. My family and I were in church, and as I opened my Bible there was your name and what you said to me that day in Iraq. I want you to know it made a difference. I had had about enough of going into danger every day without it showing any benefits, just so the commander could do a PowerPoint briefing. He didn't seem to care much about my life or my team, sending us out into danger for such trivial things."

Continuing, he said I might not remember what I had said, but he did. He had written it down that very night. He had explained how he was about ready to give up; then I had walked with him, put my arm around his shoulder, and said, "Son, everyone can't do what we do. That's why God made us strong."

He then told me, "Everything clicked, coming from you, as you went out nearly every day, unlike many of the senior officers. In so many words, you captured the situation and handed it to me. I just wanted to thank you."

Wells Parker, from Panama City, Florida, without a doubt I know you are still a good soldier for the United States. You hold your family and God first, and you believe in doing the right thing. I know you and folks like you are responsible for making this country great.

Thank you, Wells Parker, for that call on a lonely, long ago Sunday afternoon—it made my day. I know, even without that little run-in the parking lot, Wells would have gone out, completed his mission, and done his duty to the best of his abilities. But maybe those few words in the parking lot helped lighten his load.

I'm sure Wells Parker has passed along valued advice at the right time that may have made a difference. I know he did that Sunday afternoon.

If someone has touched your life in some way, let them know. It helps folks know their lives matter.

Sometimes it's the little things that matter. Godspeed, Wells Parker.

I'm a Sure Bet for Political Correctness Hell

I FIND IT DIFFICULT TO CHANGE SUBJECTS WHEN DEALING with children. Also, I realized political correctness gets in the way of childhood playing, at least playing the way I remember.

I know that in today's "progressive time," shooting firearms and teaching marksmanship to kids is taboo. Even playing with toy weapons is wrong, according to the leftists' way of thinking. But I have been known to be a little behind the times, and some might even say I'm barbaric or primitive in nature. Whatever the case may be, Morgan, age six, and I play cops and robbers; cowboys and Indians; army; bad guy versus good guy; and hunting, with his toy pistols, toy double-barreled shotgun, toy rifles, and Nerf guns. We play both outside and inside. Political correctness, stand down.

The other day we had been playing for much longer than my attention span allows. We had shot at and hit everything in the house, at least in our minds. I was running low on steam, but Morgan was going strong and winning. I was secretly trying to change games and take a break. Morgan, sensing the old man was losing or couldn't hack it anymore, changed his game and picked up the pace, all the while telling me how glad he was for me to be playing with him. He even used a little psychology on me, telling me that he didn't have anyone else to play with, which shamed me into continuing—smart kid.

As I continued trying to weasel out of playing, he was getting the quilts and blankets and asking me to help him build the biggest fort ever in the living room to provide a barrier to shoot behind. Well, he had me for a while longer. We built the fort, and I settled in for what I thought was going to be a rest period inside the fort. I was wrong.

I know that one day Morgan will get into trouble at school for picking up a stick and playing with it like it's a toy gun or using his finger to "play shoot" birds in the sky; then off to the office he will go. And it will be my primitive parenting that's let him down. And when he lets it out of the bag that he has a lifetime membership to the National Rifle Association (NRA), just like his brother, both will be doomed to socialist-sponsored retraining camps. I'm afraid I've set them both up for hard times in this world. They are also going to be labeled barbaric. It's sort of like that song about the boy named Sue. "Why did you name me Sue? Tom, Jerry, anything but Sue." I think playing with toy guns and membership in the NRA might make them tougher for the future, if they have to live in a progressive world of political correctness. Maybe, just maybe, President Trump can bring back kids playing, manners, and a little sanity to our world.

I worry about the future world our children and grandchildren will have to navigate. The world is a little different today, and political correctness has helped to do the changing.

A Young Merchant
Marine Sailor

Jerry Hatcher and I were in San Francisco, California, when "(Sittin' on) the Dock of the Bay" by Otis Redding was popular. We had just graduated from the Harry Lundeberg School of Seamanship out of New Orleans. We were two local hayseeds, freshly out of Calhoun County, entering a strange, adventure-filled new world. We had joined the merchant marines and were waiting in San Francisco to catch our first merchant ship. The Seafarers International Union (SIU) in New Orleans had paid our way to California. We had certified documents stating we were recently qualified graduates of Harry Lundeberg's school and were ready to face our first job.

We heard this song for the first time while sitting there on the Frisco Bay, waiting for our first ship. Little did we know, we faced a daunting future: long voyages across vast oceans, Vietnam, foreign countries, typhoons, loneliness, gambling, fights, union ways and dues, adventures, good money, good stories to tell, new and interesting sights. But we were always thinking of home.

And there we were, sitting on that San Francisco Bay, listening to Otis, wondering what the future held for us.

I've often felt I had a particular purpose for my life. I enjoyed and appreciated my school years. Upon graduation I went right into junior college—two semesters—and then into the merchant marines, before being drafted into the US Army. All were hidden blessings.

I was the first to ship out to Vietnam. I last saw Jerry in the union hall in San Francisco. He shipped out overseas a short while later. I didn't see Jerry again until I arrived back in Calhoun County many months later. We both had stories to tell.

As a young person of eighteen years of age, I had the good fortune to be able to explore, travel, and survive civilian adventures in Vietnam before being drafted into the army. I'll write about how it all came about later, but tonight I was writing about a wild-eyed, naive young man exploring Vietnam as a civilian in 1969.

I found myself on board a C3 freighter, the USS *Mobilian*, sailing into the harbor in Qui Khon, Vietnam. It was a bright, clear, bluebird-crisp morning. There I was, standing tall and straight on the bow, with the cool morning breeze blowing and the ocean spray fueling my imagination. We were moving into a beautiful lush, green, landscaped harbor. I had the best seat in the house.

As an eighteen-year-old, I was not mature but full of confidence, with little to no worries and a pocket full of money. I was a world traveler, a merchant seaman, not too bright, and somewhat naive, untested, but with a belief in everything good about the United States. I was and still am a believer.

Early that first morning, a sixteen-year-old first-time sailor named Phillip and I went ashore on leave. On a merchant ship, when in a harbor, there was always a week or so of off time for mariners while the vessel was off-loading and on-loading. Even if Phillip was only sixteen, he was worlds ahead of me in experience on the streets. He was from Orlando and raised very differently. Even though he was street savvy, I still had to watch out for him, more so than the other way around, which can be attributed to my upbringing and the fact he had a reckless nature.

After leaving the ship's dock and the post's gate security, we were on the road toward town, which started right outside the gates. The first new sight I saw was a process with which I was sort of familiar. A Vietnamese man had a dead, steaming dog lying on a board in front of him. The dog had just been taken out of the scalding hot water. He was scraping the hair off the dog with a sharp knife. I instantly knew what was happening—dog for lunch. I explained to Phillip what was going on and the process he was using. That gentleman was preparing the dog for cutting into meal-size pieces.

Only a few steps farther was an entirely different scene. There were three somewhat young Vietnamese ladies, squatting, one behind the other, with a little girl standing in front. They were picking something from each other's long straight black hair and then putting it into their mouths before biting down. Upon closer look, I figured they were picking out head lice and then killing them by biting them. I never saw one of them spit anything out. They may have been eating them or maybe moving them out of the side of their mouths, like someone would nut husks. I just don't know.

I had a camera but was hesitant about taking photos of people, in case they might not want me to, but now I wish I had taken more photos.

We had heard there was much racial tension within the US military at that time. We were very much aware of that. It showed in Vietnam, with apparent segregation between Black and white troops. Some streets had only Black US soldiers patrolling them, and on others there were only white soldiers. Some streets were completely abandoned, which gave us an uneasy feeling, and we stayed away.

Qui Khon Valley was a lush, green, beautiful natural harbor. Thinking back, it was as pretty a setting for a war as I have ever seen. In the huge valley was a large city, military base, and harbor. At any given time, day or night, there were dozens of aircraft to be seen. On the right, there were maybe six or eight helicopters and two or more planes flying around. To the left, the same; then there were the larger planes flying in and out of the valley. The entire valley was alive with people and activity. Mortar and/or rockets would come flying into the valley. It was a never-ending, late evening, something we got used to in Vietnam. The harbor was always bustling with large and small boats, with swift boats using grenades that explode underwater, in case a diver wanted to come into the port. It was a busy valley.

It was much bigger than Maggie Valley; the valley reached as far as I could see. Much of my time there included friendly artillery firing to some remote location from the highlands around Qui Khon.

As American civilians, we had uncontrolled access to the valley. The US government and the Vietnamese didn't know what we were. Some thought contractors, some thought a US three-letter agency, some just thought we were crazy, wandering in and around the valley, catching military convoys, taxis, scooters to and from the valley, villages, and venues. It was surreal times, and looking back a very dangerous time, but rich in experience, education, and adventure.

We were blessed.

Note: Jerry Hatcher and I followed Tommy Darrell Montford out to New Orleans in 1969 to join the merchant marines. This was during the height of the Vietnam War. Jerry and I stayed alive and were successful in going into the merchant marines, after which I was drafted into the US Army. But the adventure of riding that bus with Tommy Darrell and the weeks in New Orleans were the stuff of movies. Jerry and I were several years younger than Tommy, and he was the master of adventure, especially at that time and in those settings. As young boys, we were brash, impressionable, and not too smart, but we were willing to learn the ways of survival. Tommy Darrel was willing to lead and show us the way. Boy, were we two country boys in for a surprise. In my writing, there will be stories of the wayward boys who went out to learn and what we found when we got there. I see that worried look on Jerry's face now. Not to worry, Jerry Hatcher, you're one of the heroes, of which there are many. Tommy Darrell was a true character, and I don't think either Jerry or I would have traded places with anyone, as those were formative days of a person's life. Tommy won a place in our memories, and I thank him for that. Rest in peace, Tommy. You were someone who came along in a young person's life to help them set their course. You were certainly instrumental in helping Jerry and me start an adventure that continues on today.

FFA AND THE AMERICAN FLAG

O NE OF THE MOST REWARDING AND EDUCATIONAL
experiences of my life was the time I spent as an ag teacher
and FFA sponsor. It was during that time that I really found myself,
and in the process I found out my students really were my kids. I
constantly strove to give those young people what they needed in life
and often felt I was not up to the task.

There were so many different personalities, such a learning curve,
such different backgrounds, such innocence, such open minds that
could win the world. What was I to do? I studied hard, got there
early, and stayed late. I worked night and day to be a good teacher
and still felt like it was never enough—that they deserved so much
more than what I had to give.

Over the course of those seven years, I learned far more from my
students than they did from me. I have many, many stories to tell
about the wonderful things that happened back then, and I plan to
tell many more in future stories. But for now I'll limit it to just one.

The American flag lapel pin was something I gave out at the
FFA awards night banquet to a few members who gave more than
required. They didn't have to be a chapter officer, star student, or
contest winner. What they did have to do was more.

What I mean is that they had to do more than they were required
to, more than might be expected of them, and sometimes more than
they thought they could. These were kids who gave their time to
others, helping out and lifting up the people they met, and going
the extra mile whether anyone noticed or not. There was a lot of

recognition and praise doled out for talent, skills, and abilities. I wanted a way to honor the kids who went above and beyond, no matter if they won ribbons and badges or not.

To me, the pin was like the flag itself: a small symbol of a much larger idea. So I placed a lot of thought into who had earned it and who had not. It wasn't an "official" award, so I didn't know if it was significant to the students or not. I just knew it was to me.

One day a student came in and seemed to be very distraught. I was immediately concerned because this was a good FFA officer who was on several regional- and state-winning teams, a leader in the chapter and school. And there he stood, almost beside himself with concern.

When I asked what the problem was, the student responded in a low, humbled voice, with his eyes looking down. "Mister Barbee, I turned in all my FFA officer reports on time. I participated and helped our teams win. I did well in class and in the chapter. Why didn't I get an American flag pin?"

This was all said coming from a very hurt young man, as if he would have given up all the other FFA pins and awards he had for that flag pin. Well, I had no idea that little American flag meant so much. But here was a great student, with great social skills and a strong team spirit, who was visibly in need of a why regarding the flag.

My answer was simple. The problem was how to explain it to this outstanding member, officer, and student so that he understood. Here's what I told him as we walked back to the main school building: "It's true that your reports were very well done, on time, and probably the best ones of all. You were at all the practices, a great team member, an excellent student and member. I just hope you clearly understand what I am about to tell you. You are probably smarter than anyone on the team and maybe the most intelligent officer in the chapter, an excellent student, and you 'mix' well. You provide and show leadership.

"But you only used a small amount of yourself to do all of that. What if you gave as much of yourself as the president of the chapter did this year or one of the others who received the flag? They went way beyond themselves, beyond their capabilities. They stepped up and out and became larger than themselves."

I had no idea if he understood what I was hoping to convey, even though he said he did. I hoped all year I didn't just destroy my teacher-student relationship.

Well, I can report that the student, who always had it in him to be successful, did understand. He is accomplished in his field and has been recognized for his abilities and achievements. That little American flag lapel pin, it turns out, meant a lot more to him than I ever expected, and he earned it the next year. He carried a heavy load and brought fellow FFA members with him. The chapter excelled. We all did. He helped us become better people.

Note: The student was Jim McClellan, a superb student of life. Jim went on to college, became an officer (captain) in the US Army Reserves, and is a published author, professional writer, mentor, outdoorsman, businessman, great parent, and family man. Jim has made a very successful life, and I know he's been bringing other folks along with him. I'm honored to have spent some time with Jim McClellan.

He doesn't know it, but I learned much from watching him and my other students interact many years ago.

Jim, I hope you're okay with me writing about you. I think it's a great story of what America is all about—opportunities.

"To whom much is given, much will be required" (Luke 12:48 KJV).

LIGHTERED WOOD PROVIDES A
BLESSING IN MANY, MANY WAYS

B ONITA AND I SOMETIMES SPEND TIME OVER AT THE EDGE
of Tate's Hell in the Apalachicola National Forest. Morgan
goes with us, and we have found an unusual way to enjoy our time,
making it beneficial to our well-being in more ways than one. We all
look for lightered wood. The wood we find brings us much warmth,
not just by burning it as a fire starter but also looking for it as a united
family adventure.

Morgan keeps us smiling and enjoying nature in an entirely
different, unique kind of adventure.

Morgan loves looking for lightered wood. As a matter of fact, he
is the lightered finder and quality control person of our family. He
knows the difference in quality of different pieces of lightered or if
it's even lightered. Morgan, just as we do, loves the smell of lightered
wood. He sometimes sleeps with a top-quality piece of fat lightered
on his nightstand. He shares the smell of it with us.

When Morgan, Bonita, or I suggest going to the camp in
Orange, Florida, Morgan's thoughts always seem to go to, *Are we
going searching for lightered?* We all love to take the Jeep, our official
government permit, an axe, vests, and a full ice chest out hunting
for lightered.

Sometimes, when we go fishing or hunting, we don't always catch
or shoot something, but when we go lightered hunting we still find
it and bring some home. Now that's fun, and Morgan makes it that
much more fun.

Our routine goes something like this: We all go driving through the forest, and when Morgan spies something that looks like a downed pine tree or lightered stump he taps on my shoulder or the top of the Jeep. We stop, and I go check out the site. I bring back a chip of the wood and give it to my quality control guy, Morgan. He then gives me a nod and a wink or shakes his head from side to side to say no. If it's lightered, we maneuver closer, get out, and start preparing and loading the treasure for transporting back to camp. Then we move on, looking for more treasure.

For nonbelievers in the healing, warmth, and medical value of lightered, it's no joke. It possesses considerable power.

LONELY NIGHTS IN FOREIGN LANDS

G OOD THOUGHTS. WE OFTEN FORGET HOW WELL WE HAVE
it here in the United States and how blessed we are to live
in this country. With tonight's weather, and because I'm not ready for
sleep, I think of the very, very cold nights and some very, very hot,
some very wet and rainy, some very, very dry nights in foreign lands.
Nights where my thoughts had time to gather—to think about life
and home. It was a lonely time in my life.

During those times, I often felt terribly alone, a little lost, and
felt sorry for myself. Wondering what in the hell I was doing and
how the hell I got there, as well as how selfishly I had acted. During
those times, I dug deep, and I realized why and how. It was because
of how I was raised, the people I knew, and the great childhood I
had. In those solemn moments, in the middle of chaos, all I had to do
was realize that even when life isn't going completely our way there
are a multitude of people who are worse off in this old world—those
in third world countries, those struggling in the United States, and
those who will live and die in dire poverty.

I always reminded myself that my health was good, and I had a
great job in which I was surrounded by great people—a job in which
I could make a difference and find a nice place to live in a great
community. Sometimes problems of the world, if we dwell on them,
whether big or small or somewhere in between, whether short-lived
or long-term, they can really rob a person of happiness.

In those moments, I concentrated my thoughts on others around me, not on myself or my shortcomings, but on my soldiers, the people we were there for, and why the United States is such a great place. It's not because of our government or politicians and their motives but because of solely my motives. God led me to that place and time, and I was to make the best of it—for my family, for my soldiers, for their families, and so that we could all be better people and enjoy the blessings that had been given to us. I was rich in life, whole, and blessed, and we were made to do things that enriched our lives, our families, and to give of ourselves, to share what we were given.

Out of the Mouth of a Six-Year-Old

Today I received a book I ordered on Amazon that I am hoping will assist with Morgan's and my knot-tying training. The name of the book is *A Practical Guide to Tying Knots*. The book was lying by my computer when Morgan came home from school. He quickly noticed the book, picked it up, and looked it over, then exclaimed, "You got a book on knots."

I replied that I had purchased the book to help us with our knot tying. He glanced over at me and back at the book as he put it back down.

With a smile on his face and a pat on my back, Morgan said, "Classic, Dad. That's just classic."

I just sat there at the computer dumbfounded. What did *classic* mean, and where did that come from? What does Morgan know about the word *classic*? I then looked up the word *classic* to study all the meanings of the word.

I wanted to discuss where he learned about the word *classic*, and I still don't know if Morgan was talking about me or the book. I've never heard him use that word before, and we've never discussed it. Morgan is just beyond me. I bet I used the word *classic* several times today. What a neat, sharp word for him to learn this early.

Once again I learned something from my six-year-old.

Rode My First Two Bulls
at Fifty Years Old

I T WAS A BEAUTIFUL DAY IN HENTOWN, GEORGIA, A LITTLE community right outside Colquitt, Georgia. My family and I went up there most Sundays to the practice pens for Brandon and Jim to ride and train on bulls that were owned by Mr. Grady Harper and his wife, Peggy. Mr. Grady and his wife were the salt of the earth. All the kids, young folks, and adults thought the world of them, and I think they returned that same feeling to the people who came there almost every Sunday. I know Brandon and Jim Barbee loved it up there, and so did I. They made everyone feel right at home; it was a family affair and a positive experience for all.

We had been going for years, but this was a special day. It was Brandon Barbee's eighteenth birthday, and Jim Barbee, who was only twelve years old, and I were planning on riding our first real-life, headstrong, deadly bovine that day. Jim was used to riding young bulls, and doing quite well at it, but had never gotten on a two-thousand-pound bull before. I'm sure Jim had given this as much thought before this day as had I. We were going to climb that mountain, cross that river, and never look back. We were celebrating Brandon's eighteenth birthday, one we would all remember.

Brandon dearly loved riding bulls—the atmosphere of the arena, his fellow riders, and the performance of the bulls. Brandon loved Mr. Harper and Ms. Peggy and the entire group of fellows who practiced at the Harper Farm. He had found another passion in life. Jim and I didn't love it so much like that, but we were supporting someone we both loved dearly. Brandon brought us along, and as peer pressure and love will sometimes do, it took Jim and me for a ride.

Brandon had no idea what Jim and I had in mind that day, other than we were going to grill on the large mobile grill and celebrate his birthday at the bullpens with many of his friends and Mr. Grady's other visitors. The grill was going strong, smoking away early that morning.

The week before, Jim was going to ride a large bull and had actually gotten on one, but he decided he wasn't mentally ready and talked Brandon into letting him unseat the large beast, which suited both Brandon and myself. Jim was an excellent bull rider, but he wasn't ready and was still a little young to be riding a large bull. But it had bothered him all week, and he was in a mindset this week to ride a massive beast. I don't remember the name of the bull that day, but I bet Jim does. Jim rode the bull, with Brandon assisting with the ropes, gates, and his dismount after Jim had ridden him way past that eight-second mark. I think Jim was hesitant about how he was going to come off that bull, so he just stayed on and kept riding until Brandon, the bullfighter, and other cowboys went to his rescue. When they came upon the bull, Jim sailed off into Brandon's arms. What a day, and it wasn't over yet.

After five or six others rode practice bulls that day, it was time for the big boy, the daddy of bulls, which was over two thousand pounds and a foot taller than the other bulls that had come into the chutes that day. I said to the young men around me, "There he is. I'll ride that one." I had kept my intentions secret from Brandon and Jim, but the other young fellows knew what I had in mind. Along with riding a bull that day, I had in mind to present Brandon with a new pair of boots I had purchased, but his girlfriend had forgotten them at home. My plans were to wear his new boots while trying to ride this bull and to present them to Brandon afterward, along with a little "daddy talk." But it didn't work out that way. I had to borrow someone's boots back behind the chutes, just before climbing over into the chute and onto the bull. By the way, I will never forget the name of that bull. He was the only bull I was ever to ride, and yes, I remember I said two bulls. Well, old Hollywood was my first bull and my last one. That makes two.

I always hesitated to try bull riding at my age. I didn't want to look foolish. I didn't want to embarrass the boys or myself. Why would anyone over twenty-five get on the back of a bull that had every intention of doing in the rider? But that day I used Brandon's birthday as my excuse to try to ride a bull. I told myself that I was doing it for Brandon and Jim, which was only part of it. It was something I had wanted to try for a while. I was still in pretty good shape for fifty years old. After all, I was an Army Ranger, and I knew I could do it, or so I kept telling myself.

Something I can say about bull riding, even with the limited experience I've had, is that it does something to one's senses, much like in combat. A person's sense of smell, hearing, feeling, apprehension, determination, emotions, are decisively enhanced.

When I climbed into the chute and sat down on the bull, I asked some of the guys to call Brandon over. He had walked over to the grill area; he didn't know what crazy Daddy was up to. Jim was standing by. Brandon appeared to me and said, "Daddy, let me pull the rope."

I remember it all like it was yesterday. Brandon pulled the rope very tight, which was around the bull, with my fingers underneath. I said, "Son, that's too tight."

He replied, "It's supposed to be tight."

I nodded as I took the final wrap and tuck.

Now, to say I was prepared for what was about to happen is a stretch. I was still in fairly good shape. I had watched enough of the boys riding and heard all the stories, and I had thought through all the things people had said to do. I was ready, and with excitement I slapped the bull beside the neck with my free balance hand. At the time I felt like it would look kind of cool, but all it did was badly sting my hand. To make matters worse, I did it again, thinking I was sending the message to him to give it all he had because this was going to be my first and last bull ride. Jim asked me later why I did that, and that's the explanation I told him.

Brandon then asked if I was ready, and I nodded and said plainly, "Give him to me." The gate was opened, and out we went into the surreal world of bull riding, just me and Hollywood. I don't claim to be a balance expert or a bull rider, but on that day God chose Mr. Hamburger Bull, Hollywood, and me to put on a show. A fifty-year-old daddy rode his first-ever bull and stayed on for the buzzer and longer, just as Jim had done. When that buzzer went off, I started to let go of the rope, but something went through my mind, probably about the same thoughts that had gone through Jim's mind a few bulls earlier. I had thought about nearly all aspects of bull riding except how to exit the bull. There was no stirrup, so I had to let the bull throw me off after turning the rope loose. I, like Jim, rode on for an eternity, four more seconds, but there was no one there to help me off, so twelve seconds into that jumping, bucking ride I had to experience that last part of bull riding. I let go.

I didn't own a cowboy hat, so that day I was wearing a cap. As I was getting up from the dirt and getting away from the bull, there came a black cowboy hat flying out into the arena and landing at my feet. I immediately recognized it as Brandon's, and as I was picking it up I took off my cap, then put the hat on. Brandon ran out to where

I was standing in the arena, stood beside me, put his arm around my shoulders, and we walked out of the arena together. While we were exiting, I gave Brandon my modified birthday talk. I said, "I see why you do this now. I hope one day when you have children you will be there for them. I love you." As we climbed the fence together, the crowd went wild, and I just grinned. That was a glorious day filled with memories.

Thank You, God, for giving me those twelve seconds and that wonderful day. Jim Barbee and I will never, ever forget that day.

Many an adventure was had with my sons while following Brandon and his passions. Today Jim and I love bow hunting, watching rodeos, fishing, and remembering Brandon's larger-than-life smile.

Note: I think Hollywood went to the hamburger house after that day. He was the biggest, slowest, and least muscled-up bull I saw that day. I've got a good eye for slow, easygoing old bulls.

Sometimes it's the right time, the right place. Sometimes it's the luck of the draw. God gave me both.

Thankful for Dogwood Trees

FIVE YEARS AGO, WHEN MORGAN WAS STILL IN DIAPERS, HE was in his infant car seat when I ran off the edge of a dirt road in a national forest, hit a tree, and totaled my truck. The truck struck about a six- to eight-inch diameter dogwood tree and slowed us down before hitting a large pine tree head-on. The pine tree stopped us. I had my hand on Morgan in his backward-facing car seat beside me, and God had his hand on both of us because Morgan's airbag was turned off, and he was all buckled in.

While the glass was still falling from the back glass and windshield, the smoke stream from the busted radiator was rising. Morgan was laughing, and I was momentarily in scared shock for my baby, who seemed to want to do it again, whatever it was we just did. I saw that Morgan was okay, so with my bruised knees I unbuckled my seat belt, kicked my stuck door open, quietly went around, and attempted to open the door to get Morgan out. Thankfully, it opened just fine. Holding Morgan tightly, I said a little prayer of thanks as we backed out away from the vehicle, in case the truck caught fire.

I called Bonita, who was working in Marianna on that weekend day, as she was on call. I told her what happened and that we were okay. I then opened the tailgate of the truck, and Morgan and I waited. Bonita beat the highway patrol to the accident. I'm sure God had his hand on her as well. We all had a little reunion, there in the forest, sitting on the tailgate.

Later, Jim, my middle boy, gave me his old truck so I would have something to drive. I'm still driving it to this day, and I've never replaced the wrecked truck.

Morgan says he doesn't remember that day. I told him that was a blessed day, and God was looking out for us. I still point out the tree and the location of the accident when we happen to drive by. That was the prettiest dogwood tree in the forest, which slowed us down before we went head-on into an immovable large pine tree.

The Gift

O VER TWELVE YEARS AGO, BRUCE MCCORMICK, A RETIRED Navy SEAL and special warfare combatant-craft crewman, and I put together a special operations training center here in the Panhandle of Florida, which was housed at the local airport. The training and activities were well received by the local and surrounding counties. The venture proved to be very successful.

After several years Bruce wanted to retire again, so the facility and plans were sold to a group of veteran special operator contractors who developed the program and expanded the training area. The facility has actually been sold several times over the years, and at first I stayed on as an advisor, at their request, to aid in their success.

One day Jim Barbee, my youngest son at the time, stopped by the facility to see it and to check on the training, and the operators caught me off guard. They called about thirty of their personnel together and had a little ceremony, gave a speech, and presented me with a special present. When they handed me the weapon and made their remarks, I had to say a few words. I thanked them and assured them that wasn't necessary, but it was much appreciated. I handed the scoped rifle over to Jim and said I hunted with a spear now, but I would give it a try. It was a neat day to share with Jim.

My reason for telling this story is what happened next. After the informal ceremony, Jim and I left and were riding back to town. Jim was admiring the weapon, an expensive Leopold scope mounted on a .300 Winchester Magnum sniper rifle that donned a thank-you plate commemorating my service. I could tell Jim was smitten with the rifle, so I told him it was his. After all, what use did I have for it at that time? After much grinning and thanking me, he went back to checking out everything on the rifle. After a few minutes, I asked Jim, "What kind of game are you going to shoot with a three hundred Winchester mag rifle?"

Jim looked kind of startled, a look that told me that he thought I should know the answer to such a silly question, and then he said words I'll never forget: "You can shoot anything you want to with this rifle."

Well, that satisfied me as I beamed at his answer. I was proud of this day with my boy.

Note: I think Jim hunts elk with it. I'm glad I made that decision that day, as it was a perfect moment. I bet Jim will hang on to that weapon and hand it down to someone. Jim has a few other weapons that all have stories behind them as well: three sniper rifles and a pistol or two from overseas. Maybe I'll get a chance to write about those one sleepless night. I love my boys. Good night.

Fourteen-Year-Olds versus the US Navy SEALs

T HERE IS A TIME IN EVERY YOUNG PERSON'S LIFE WHEN THEY do something they will always remember. This is a story about a group of fourteen-year-olds from Calhoun County and a time they will never forget.

Several years before this story began, Bruce McCormick and I put together a special operations training program in Calhoun County. The program turned into a training center at the Blountstown Airport, located along Highway 71. It became a place that hosted many interesting training exercises. This is a story of one of those programs.

Over the years many training exercises have taken place in Calhoun and Liberty counties involving special operators with the US military, but this particular one got the most publicity. Bruce invited and set up a training opportunity with a West Coast Navy SEALs detachment for training in the Florida Panhandle. I was responsible for some of the training they were to experience, and I was determined to make it unique. I've always found that if one imprints people with an extraordinary experience they will never forget it. It will be something they will talk about throughout their lives, something meaningful and worthy of their time. Participants were local young men, ladies, and the famous US Navy SEALs.

Bruce's determination for this type of training in the Panhandle wasn't based strictly on financial gains; he was a highly patriotic person who had a passion for our military. My interests, on the other hand, were to help bring economic development to our small part of the world without changing our southern lifestyle. I also have high regard for the training of our troops, and more importantly I wanted our kids to see, experience, talk to, and aspire to become someone who achieves in this earthly world. Having a certain caliber of young American patriots here training locally would hopefully mean Calhoun and Liberty youth would see that they, too, could obtain this type of success. America is a land where one can set goals and become anything they want to be.

I suggested to Bruce that we create a few unique training events that would imprint on this group so they would want to come back again and again. Bruce bought into some of my suggestions, and off we went. First, I solicited a little help. I asked my son Jim if he would get together twelve or so young people who he knew with woods experience, owned climbing stands, camo, etc. They were to become the local partisan Rangers, who were going to work as the opposing forces. Bruce told the SEALs he had US Army Rangers coming over to operate against them, from over at the training center at Eglin Air Force Base, and they didn't play around.

Then I contacted the local sheriff, David Tatum, and he was as energizing as always, with a great imagination. He became a player in training. Sheriff Tatum booked several department of corrections tracking teams from around the Panhandle. He made dog-barking cassette tapes, and as always he played an important role in helping to train these new visitors to our county. Calhoun County had a surprise for our new visitors: world-class training.

We had to have an inside man to help the opposing forces (OPFOR) do their job, so Bruce hired Jim to wash dishes and do odd jobs around their housing area. Bruce had leased the J&N building along Highway 20, west of Blountstown, to house, feed, and conduct operations. He also leased the old shipyard, the 4-H cabins in the park, and hired a local to prepare meals. Jim became our eyes and ears for the OPFOR, trying to find out relevant information that would be helpful for the training of good, solid Navy SEAL teams. Of note, Jim never got caught doing undercover work.

One training event the SEALs and boat specialists were doing was an escape and evade exercise. This was one of the activities we had planned. We were ready.

The navy personnel dropped by teams of two along several stretches of the Apalachicola River. The river table was very high, around twenty feet or more. The mission was to swim the river through the backwater, escape and evade the enemy, and make it across Highway 69 south without being seen or captured.

The OPFOR personnel—our twelve fourteen-year-olds, the dog handlers, dogs, and local authorities—were to find them and stop them. The young men, dressed in camo, brought their climbing stands, a battery-operated boom box, and a handheld radio. They were to be trail watchers, boom box players, photo takers, and lookouts. David Tatum was in charge of the youth team, dog handlers, and local authorities. Early that morning he briefed them and went over the plans; then they were all dropped off to take their stands and to be ready. After all, this was the United States Navy SEALs they were up against, but all were confident and ready to perform.

The SEALs had never had dogs on their tails before, and so their training fell short related to how to react when dogs were involved. Even though they knew there would be dogs, one thing they didn't know was these tracking dogs don't bark while trailing. The OPFOR was strung out up and down Highway 69 south at designated spots, in elevated positions in trees, to "capture" the SEALs when and if they came through their area. But they also had another mission:

to activate the boom boxes with the prerecorded sounds of dogs barking at the appropriate time. The plan was to fool the escapees into thinking they were running into dogs on their front so they would turn around and run into the trackers with the silent dogs. If nothing else, it was a delaying tactic, and it worked. Most were captured by the dog teams and caught on photos by the trail watchers.

Something we didn't figure on was the imagination, the tenacity, the aggressive nature of our youth on this little training exercise. Some of the youth were able to capture closeup photos of the escapees emerging from the backwater. One even took his video camera and followed two escapees, taping the entire way as they crawled through a couple of culverts under Highway 69 south, attempting to make their way to safety. He filmed them sitting under a tree, talking after they crossed the road. I asked the young fellow why he didn't get close enough to get good sound, and he responded, "Sir, are you crazy? They are Navy SEALs." He had no idea how well he had done, even without orders to do so.

The guys in training and their officers and NCOs learned much from the unique training they acquired here in the Panhandle, and believe it or not they were not upset that many of them had been compromised by a group of young southern boys. As a matter of fact, they were impressed and praised the boys and their effort. The trainees had learned much and were world class about it.

We all learned and all had stories to tell. Some of those youngsters, in their years after high school, went into the military, and others took the lessons they learned and grew with them.

All our training and goals for such training here in the Panhandle were met and surpassed. Bruce and I went home after this training event with all our hopes for a successful event fulfilled. We have a great community and great folks. How about that for a story to be told?

Note: I wished I had taken and saved photos of the event, but I didn't. I'm betting there are some out there somewhere though.

Also, the moms and dads of the young folks who came out to see the SEALs in training seemed to like the idea that we had conducted the training here locally. And by the number of single ladies who gathered up out on Highway 71, near J&N, in the evenings, watching the SEALs complete their evening fitness training, I'd say the mission was successful. The SEALs' training captured Calhoun and Liberty counties' imagination.

WHERE IS THE FRUIT?

FOR MOST OF MY LIFE I HAVE TRIED TO EXPLAIN TO FOLKS that the fruit of life is attained when one sets and achieves their goals. Many people over the years have commented, "Why would anyone jump out of a perfectly good airplane? Why would anyone want to subject themselves to such punishment by pursuing the Ranger tap? Why did you go into the merchant marines? Why would you ever want to go to college? Why would you become an underwater diver? Why would you volunteer for such an assignment? Why? Why? Why?"

Why would anyone do something out of the ordinary, something others might not see themselves doing? Well, my answer for such a question has always been: That's where the fruit is located, at least for me. Now your fruit may be in a different location than mine. It seems that everyone has different tastes in life, and the arena in which we choose to play is not always for all people.

On my first tour of Iraq, I became interested in that country's date industry and studied their date palm trees whenever I got an opportunity. While some folks were taking a break or had time off, I was up in a date palm tree or talking with locals about their palm trees. Some of my peers found it odd—funny, maybe—of me, at that time a colonel in the US Army, to be climbing palm trees. Well, my curiosity served me well. During my tenure in Iraq, I helped start the National Date Palm Rejuvenation Campaign led by their minister of agriculture, Dr. Salsum. Dates in Iraq are known to be the best in the world and had been their number two world-exported commodity, right behind oil, their number one export.

Some of my soldiers used to see me up in different date palm trees in the vicinity of our living quarters. I used the locals' method of climbing and securing dates with a strap made of palm thatch, rope, and a machete. I would then lower down bundles of dates. They would stop by, and I would share the fresh dates. Some would always ask, "Sir, why do you climb those trees?"

Well, to me, that was a simple answer, but I couldn't explain it well enough for them to understand in their language, so I simply stated, "That's where the fruit is at."

There are over five hundred varieties of date palm trees, and most come out of Iraq. Iraq has ten varieties that are the very best in the world. The type of date that Saddam liked best was not let out for export; however, they are now growing in Calhoun and Liberty counties. Several locals have them growing on their property; I can't wait until they start producing. Those date palms grow tall, majestic, and are magnificent palms, with a little history behind them. Saddam once owned them on his palace grounds, and the seeds were taken from those trees. This variety of palms may actually be the only ones in the world outside Iraq.

Florida has the same climactic latitude as Iraq. Even though they are dry, and we are wet, our zones are the same. The dry conditions are best for dates, but we should be able to produce many good dates from the palms as they mature.

During my first deployment to Iraq, one of the areas I worked was out in the red zone, as a lone advisor to several of the Iraqi ministries. I had the pleasure of assisting, advising, learning, studying, and teaching at several Iraqi agriculture universities and the Iraqi ministry research institutions. When the Iraqis heard about my study of their beloved date palm trees, and that I actually climbed them myself, they were taken aback but showed great respect for the honor I placed on their favorite tree. They knew I had genuine interest and showed respect, beyond just doing my job. Because of this, I was one of the only senior advisors, and the prime minister allowed me to stay in the field when all other advisors were pulled out

About three weeks before being redeployed back to the States, all personnel were swelled with excitement about going back home. All our soldiers, as well myself, were thinking more of what we needed to do or wanted to do when we got back. Several soldiers had heard I had mentored others into parachuting back into the States, so several came to me to say that was something they wanted to do upon returning home. They had many questions about skydiving and parachuting, and one soldier, a young sergeant, said he wanted his first jump to be at least ten thousand feet. Doing that on a first jump is plenty unusual, and before I knew it I asked why on earth he would want to do that. The young sergeant stepped back and smiled. He simply stated, "Sir, that's where my fruit is at."

After returning from Iraq, that young sergeant made his first jump, in Quincy, Florida, at the School of Human Flight, along with several other young soldiers. I was watching, just grinning, as they sailed out of the plane.

Upon my retirement from the military, after a short ceremony, I had an opportunity to say a few words. I told them the date palm story and joked about how my peers made light of my climbing those tall palm trees. And I concluded with, "If anyone ever asks you why you joined up or why you did or are doing something in particular, here's your answer."

I then called on the young sergeant by name to answer. He shouted, "That's where the fruit is at!"

I saluted the soldiers and retired with a smile. God Bless our military.

350TH CIVIL AFFAIRS COMMAND

COMBAT PATCH AWARD

Let it be known that you, Colonel Logan B. Barbee, USAR, have been presented with this award of the United States Army Civil Affairs and Psychological Operations Command (USACAPOC) Combat Patch in recognition of your contributions to the Multi-National Force-Iraq, the 350th Civil Affairs Command, and the Iraqi people, while deployed in support of Operation Iraqi Freedom. Your efforts reflect great credit upon yourself, the United States Army Reserve and serves as an example for all of the people of Iraq. Thank you for a job well done.

Given this, the 21st Day of September, 2004, In Baghdad, Iraq

Charles H. Davidson, IV
Brigadier General, USA
Commanding

If anyone in the old 350th's first deployment to Iraq in 2003 would like to hear the story behind the SSPP (Super Secret Pigeon Project) versus the Units Never Dying Power Point, there is definitely a story to be told. Maybe enough time has passed to tell it. I have a good Power Point brief. At the time, heads would have rolled, but the pigeons worked.

Systems Functionality	
CAKMS	**JSSPP**
• High tech military geopolitical stuff • Can solve world hunger (with add on modules) • Not for use with computers • Still working on ability to bring dead back to life	• Low maintenance • Self-replicating • Reliably used for many centuries • Always return home • Effective NBC early warning system • Can be an emergency food source

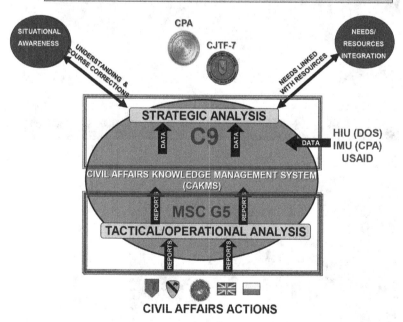

Back row: Dr. Rob Gene Parrish, LTC and Logan Barbee, COL. Front row: Danny Hassig, MAJ. This picture of us with "the hog" was taken outside my billet. The boar head was always grinning. Sometimes, I think the boar head had a grander time than we did. Many soldiers wanted a picture with "the hog." I kept an array of captured weapons to use to secure our compound and for the occasional photo session.

Logan Barbee

THE UNITED STATES OF AMERICA

TO ALL WHO SHALL SEE THESE PRESENTS, GREETING: THIS IS TO CERTIFY THAT THE PRESIDENT
OF THE UNITED STATES OF AMERICA AUTHORIZED BY ACT OF CONGRESS 20 JULY 1942 HAS AWARDED

THE LEGION OF MERIT

TO

COLONEL LOGAN B. BARBEE
UNITED STATES ARMY

FOR exceptionally meritorious service from 14 December 1994 to 13 December 2004 in various positions of increasing responsibility. His tenure as the Assistant Chief of Staff, G-2, 350th Civil Affairs Command, highlights 30 years of distinguished service. Colonel Barbee's organizational abilities and expertise in agricultural affairs made him a highly sought after Soldier. He has served the Civil Affairs Community and the United States Army admirably and with distinction. His extraordinary achievements throughout his military career reflect distinct credit upon himself, the United States Army Civil Affairs and Psychological Operations Command (Airborne), the United States Army Special Operations Command, and the United States Army.

BY ORDER OF THE SECRETARY OF THE ARMY

THIS 4TH DAY OF AUGUST 2004

PO 217-1, 4 August 2004
HQ, USASOC
Fort Bragg, North Carolina 28310

PHILIP R. KENSINGER, JR.
Lieutenant General, USA
Commanding

DA FORM 4980-11, JUL 2003. Previous edition is obsolete

| 46 |

My middle son, Brandon's, basic training photo. He was hoping to go to ranger school and was due to graduate and receive a commission from the ROTC within a year. One day, I asked Brandon why he wanted to go into the rangers. I thought he may have wanted to follow in his father's footsteps. But no, Brandon thought being a ranger would help him be a better bull rider, and it would have. I loved his answer. Rest in peace, son. We miss you.

BRANDON B. BARBEE
U S Army, Ft. Benning, GA
Aug. 12, 2001

Ole Clyde and Joe Woods' cousin had my back that day. Clyde and I were on a little side tour of the camp and looked up Joe's cousin who worked with blackwater all the time. Clyde hasn't told anyone everything he did in Iraq. He isn't just a plumber; Clyde has many skills.

Matthew, Brandon, Jim, and I were blessed to take Dad to the naval air station in Panama City, Florida, years ago when seven Pearl Harbor survivors were presented with medals. It was a momentous occasion for the boys and me, but my dad seemed far away in his thoughts that day. He didn't talk much about the war. We were all proud, and I'm glad we were there with him. I wish I could find the photos of that day. He was just seventeen years old on December 7, 1941. He woke up to history being made that day. I hope the boys remember and understand.

BUSTER BROWNIE BARBEE
CPO, U S Navy, WW II
Pearl Harbor Survivor

In 1973, I graduated from ranger School and made it home in

time for the start of bow season in North Florida. I killed my first buck and the bobcat pictured below with my bear recurve (Kodak hunter).There were only one or two people in the county that hunted with a bow and arrow in those days. The only person to ever kill a deer, at least that I'd heard of, was a game warden who has since been relocated to another county. Tree stand bow holders were new and we'd only heard of them in a few magazines. No one I knew of at the time baited deer. I hunted on the edges of soybean fields. I would set my bow on a big limb in the biggest tree I could find.

My boys and I spent many years bow hunting. Jim still hunts, and I hope Morgan will do the same. (Morgan turned nine the year this book was published.)

The boar's head from the Panhandle of Florida, welcoming everyone that day to the first International Invitational Iraqi Archery Championship. The head has a great morale booster for the troops. Hundreds participated from twelve different countries. They gave away thousands of dollars in prizes, all donated by America.

If I Were Giving
Advice to Myself

N O REGRETS.
Find your way doing things you love.

Then keep moving ahead. Grow, do, see, get there early, and stay the course. Keep your eyes open, and don't let peer pressure rule you. Do what you think is best for you and your family.

Communicate and seek advice—sometimes.

Make the most out of what you are dealt and stay positive. Try to do your best, for yourself and others. See where your life leads and make the best of it. You're the only one who can do it, and we only have one shot.

Try not to have many regrets.

Everyone can't do what we do. That's why God made us strong.

Tinker, Sailor, Soldier, Educator, County Agent, Special Agent, Spy

A S THE HEADING SUGGESTS, I'VE LIVED A VARIED, FOREVER-challenging, exciting life. I learned the electrical, plumbing, and structural building trades from my father while in grade school. I joined the US Merchant Marines and then was drafted into the US Army, where I volunteered to be schooled, trained, and assigned as a US Army Ranger. Then I was schooled and university educated as a teacher of agriculture and received my commission as an army officer. As a military officer, my assignments included military intelligence, counterintelligence, intelligence agent, chemical officer, and civil affairs officer. I then trained and worked overseas in a civilian capacity as a senior advisor to the US State Department and US Department of Agriculture. Then, once eligible to do so, I retired from the University of Florida; the US Army, at the rank of colonel; and the US State Department (GS-15). After retirement, I kept busy with consulting and contracting work.

I developed a certain degree of proficiency in all the above areas and gained invaluable experiences. All those duties were well-suited for my active personality and degree of motivation. I enjoyed all my experiences and took pride in the accomplishments those opportunities made possible. I've often thought I was chosen as a candidate for intelligence operations because of my varied background and training. These made for great cover stories and identities. I was an old southern boy covered with an accent and a few unique skills.

I trained a lot, studied continually, and worked more than one job almost all my life. I kept busy, and I'm continuing to do so in retirement.

If one ever wonders how or why I did all these activities, my answer would be, "That's what life handed me, and that's what I accepted." Those things in life that I did get to choose—somewhat—were choices that went along with raising a family and living life. While celebrating life to its fullest and fulfilling obligations, one has to make decisions, sometimes quickly. Even though my decisions weren't always the best, I find myself content and pleased with most of my major life choices.

I guess my reason for writing this chapter is to try to help those closest to me—and any others who might find it of interest—to get a little understanding about how I got to where I am and who I am.

Rangers lead the way.

Billy Blackman, writer, logger, railroad man, farrier, and folk legend from Wewahitchka, Florida, once wrote something I'll never forget and that I have told others many, many times.

Billy told me—and I'll try and get it right—that when he and his mother traveled down that road she held his hand tight, showing him right, and he tried and tried to pull away many times, but she held tight. One day, when they came to a fork in the road, he was able to pull away. Then Billy said, "Mother never blamed the little boy nor the devil, but she did blame Eddie, my cousin."

I don't know who my folks could blame for my decisions. If they disagreed with them, only I was to blame. I chose the path I thought was laid out for me. That's where my fruit was located to keep me going, or so I thought. There were other forks in the road, also gates and doors that opened.

But I didn't choose them. I think I did the best I could with what I was handed.

I hope so.

Logan Barbee

BIOGRAPHICAL SUMMARY

January 2004
Barbee, Logan Browning XXX-XX-XXXX
Col., Civil Affairs, USAR
Date and Place of Birth: 12 April 1949, Quincy, FL Hospital
MRD: 01 Mar 2005
Home Address: P O Box 84, Blountstown, FL 32424
Present Assignment: Team Chief (06) of Civil Affairs Command
Economics and Commerce Section
Civilian Occupation: Agricultural Extension Director
USDA-University of Florida
(see attached addendum)
Enlisted Service: 2 years-Draftee-RA 1969–1971
Source and Date of Commission: ROTC, 13 December 1974
Years Total Federal Officer Service: 24 years
Military Schools attended:
USA Engr Sch, Powerman Crs, 7wks, 69
USA Engr Sch, Pre Pwr Gen OM, 4wks, 69
Ranger Crs, USAIA, 10wks, 73
ROTC, FLA A & M Univ, 72–74
USAICS, MI OBC, 9wks, 75
5th USAAIS, Counterintelligence
Officer/Tech/Agent, 36A, 55 days, 76
Graduated Chemical Advance Course, 83
Graduated Military Intelligence Advance Course, 89
Graduated Civil Affairs Advance Course, 94
Graduated Command & General Staff Course, 94
Graduated Security Managers Course, 40 hrs, 98

Air War College (AWC), Tyndall AFB, (50% completed)
Civilian Education: Graduate, HSD, Blountstown High School
Blountstown, Florida 67
Graduate, Harry Lundeberg School of Seamanship, New Orleans, LA, 69
Graduate, AA, Chipola Jr. College, Marianna, FL, 72
Graduate, BS, Agriculture/Business,
FLA A & M University, Tallahassee, FL, 74
Graduate, MS, Adm/Supervision, University of West
Florida, Pensacola, FL,
US Decorations/Badges: LM The Legion of Merit
BSM Bronze Star Medal
DMSM Defense Meritorious Service Medal
JSCM Joint Service Commendation Medal
ARCOM Army Commendation Medal-5
GCM Army Good Conduct Medal
ARCAM Army Reserve Comp Achievement Medal-4
NDSM National Defense Service Medal-2
AFEM Armed Forces Expeditionary Medal
VSM Vietnam Service Medal
AFSM Armed Forces Services Medal
AFRM Armed Forces Reserve Medal ASR Army Service Ribbon
OSR Overseas Service Ribbon-2
NATOM North Atlantic Treaty Organization Medal
RGRT Ranger Tab
CAB Combat Action Badge
Chronological List of Appointments:
2LT USAR 13Dec74
1LT USAR 12Dec77
CPT USAR 11Dec81

MAJ USAR 10DEC89

LTC USAR 15SEP94

Col USAR 15OCT99

Military Assignments: Germany (enlisted-RA), 69–71

USAR Control Group Annual Training, 75

USAR Control Reinforcement, 75–76

519th MI BN (Aug) Fort Bragg, NC

Counterintelligence Off/Spec Agt/Technician 120th ARCOM, 76–77

USAR Control Group Standby, 78–80

Commander of 463rd CM Det (Decon), Panama City, FL, Jan 80–Aug 80

Commander of 425th CM Det (Decon), Panama City, FL, 80–82

West Point Military Academy, Liaison Officer, 84–86

Commander of 428th CM Det, Tallahassee, FL, 86–88

Commander of 425th CM Det, (NBCE), Panama City, FL, 88–91

USAR Control Group Standby, 91–92

361st CA Bde, Pensacola, FL, Agricultural Officer, Nov 91–95

G-2 Staff, 95–96

G-2 Assistant Chief of Staff, 96–98

Deployed to Bosnia, 361st CA Bde, Nov96–Jul97, (8 months) as Assistant Chief of Staff, G-2 350th CA Cmd, Pensacola, FL

G-2 Assistant Chief of Staff, Jul97–Aug99

350th CA Cmd, Pensacola, FL

Team Chief, Economics and Commerce Section Aug

Jun01–Jun03
G-2 Assistant Chief of Staff, Jun 03 to present
Agricultural Officer—Ministry of Agriculture
Coalition Prov. Authority (CPA), Iraqi
Reconstruction Office (IRMO)
Baghdad, Iraq November 2003–Oct 2004

ADDENDUM TO BIOGRAPHICAL SUMMARY

BARBEE, Logan Browning XXX-XX-XXXX

Civilian Occupation: Agriculture Extension Agent/Director, 1981–2005

Overall administrative/supervisory

responsibility for 5–6 member staff.

Perform agriculture and field education

for agronomic crops, livestock, alternative

crops and community economic development

projects. Work cooperatively with all phases

local, state and federal agencies. University of Florida-USDA

Employee

Specialty—Community and Rural Development

Owner, Coastal Foam, Inc., manufacturer of

Polystyrene foam for insulation, packaging,

flotation, block fill, structured.

Co-owner, River Valley Seafoods, Inc., processor

of seafood—packaging, processing—private

label packaging, custom processing. Civilian Special Skills/

Background:

Agricultural Instructor, 8 years experience,

youth and adult education. 18 years

University

Private Construction Contractor (certified)

6 years experience

Electrician/Plumber (certified) 15 years

Sports Parachutist

Diver, International Certification, open water

Merchant Seaman, card holder-Seafarers
International Union
Business Development Consultant—12 years
Agricultural Advisor—8 years

Military Occupation Specialties:
Military Intelligence/Counterintelligence
Officer—Branch Qualified
Chemical Officer—Branch Qualified
Civil Affairs Officer—Branch Qualified
Additional Skills Identifiers:
US Army Ranger (5R)
Agricultural Officer (6U)
Civil Defense Officer (5Y)
Public Education Officer (6D)
Officially, retired 2005. Deployed back to Iraq with the US State
Department as a Senior Field Advisor.

A Profile of Duty, Honor, and Country: The Danny Hassig Story

I DIDN'T KNOW DANNY HASSIG WELL IN HIS EARLY YEARS. HE didn't take my classes back when I was teaching high school, but he, like many others, did come to me for advice from time to time. Most times it was to talk about the military and what kind of jobs and opportunities they offered.

That's always been a subject I take very seriously, especially as I talked with young people about their lives and their careers. Patriotism, courage, love of country, and service to others are among the values I have most respected in people in general and in young Americans in particular. So I try to share my experiences and encourage those, like Danny, who were willing to make the sacrifices it takes to wear the uniform.

Back then, and still today, I treat all these young people like they're my own. I stand by what I say, and I've never second-guessed myself on the advice I gave, solicited or not, but something happened in Danny's case that took me off guard.

Years after leaving my teaching job at Blountstown High School, I was working for the University of Florida as the Calhoun County extension agent. One day I got a call from a lady I didn't know very well at the time.

"I don't know whether to be mad at you or not," said the voice on the other end of the line. "My son joined the army, and you told him to volunteer for everything."

I couldn't argue. That sure sounded like something I would say.

"Other folks told him to not volunteer for anything," she continued, "but he listened to you, and he's been jumping out of airplanes, shooting machine guns, and volunteering for all sorts of things. Danny wanted me to call to let you know something."

At that point I figured she must be Danny Hassig's mother, and I was holding my breath, wondering what might have happened. After a long moment of silence, she continued. "He's been selected as the soldier of the year at Fort Bragg, North Carolina."

I relaxed a little. I could tell Mrs. Gail O'Bryan had been a worried mother, as most of them are, but I could hear in her voice that she was a very proud mother as well, as she should've been.

Making soldier of the year is a great honor anywhere, but especially at Fort Bragg, where so many of the nation's most elite troops and units are stationed. I was proud as well. Here was a young man from a small town in the Florida Panhandle, distinguishing himself among the cream of the United States Army.

I thought back on the things I had talked about with Danny—the same things I would later tell my son Brandon. We had talked a lot about what it means to be a patriot, about stepping up and doing what's right, about staying positive no matter the circumstances, and about living by the following motto: if others can do it, so can we.

We talked about growing personally and climbing higher on life's ladder so that we can get a better view—and so that we can lift up others coming behind us.

I don't know whether Danny ever took any of my advice, but I do know he was raised right and that he has lived a full, multidimensional, adventure-filled life.

This is all from my perspective and what I have seen from where

I sit. Honestly, though, I don't know how anybody could see it differently.

Soon after leaving Fort Bragg and active service, Danny enrolled at a small college in North Carolina, where he took ROTC, graduated, and received his commission as an officer in the military intelligence branch. When he volunteered to return to active duty, now as a second lieutenant, he was also Airborne and air-assault qualified, with meaningful and honorable enlisted experience behind him.

I didn't see Danny for several years, but I always kept track of him through his mom, Mrs. Gail. I know he served overseas in Korea, made captain, and then left the service for civilian employment. After that, I didn't hear from him for about five years.

I don't remember exactly how we reconnected, whether I contacted Danny or if he stopped by my office, but I do remember working to get him to come back into the army—this time as a reservist in the civil affairs unit, where I served as chief of intelligence.

Danny was a prime candidate for the type of work we did. Among the most-deployed units—active and reserve—in the US military, ours was made up of people who were successful in both civilian and military life. We needed outstanding soldiers who brought to the military other professional skills as well.

Danny had been out of the service for five years, but once again he volunteered. Over the course of several years in the unit, he held a variety of jobs because we wanted people to have different experiences and develop new skills. As I expected, he thrived in that environment and proved himself during several real-world missions.

Shortly before the start of the second war in Iraq, Operation Iraqi Freedom, Danny was called up to go with a team from our unit into Hungary. There he was to set up a program to train Iraqi American citizens for service if and when the war started.

As the troop buildup began for the invasion, Danny and the soldiers he was training were transferred to Kuwait. They would go into Iraq with the main invasion task force.

As I remember it, Danny was concerned because his team of thirty or so Iraqis was deploying with the 101 Airborne Division, but nobody seemed to know what their mission would be. About halfway to Baghdad, he finally got a chance to address this problem with the division commander.

I'm sure the commander of the 101st had no idea what an asset he had in his command—in Danny or in the team he had built. The general was just invading and moving toward Baghdad to get Saddam and his regime out of power. But he had no interpreters and no one who understood the realities of life in the territory—no one other than the people Danny trained.

I suspect he was surprised and overjoyed to find out Danny had thirty people who could speak the language, who knew the area, who were willing to do whatever was needed and, most importantly, who were US citizens. As a result, the Iraqis were put into key positions throughout the command and proved to be a valuable asset in the invasion.

Right after that meeting, however, Danny and the other soldiers from our unit were recalled back to the States. That's right—halfway to Baghdad, they were brought back home.

It just so happened that at the very same time the rest of our unit was being called up to go into Iraq as the first follow. So, when Danny got home, he immediately volunteered to go back with us even though he was just coming off a yearlong deployment.

As for the rest of us, we were in the premobilization phase, still in Pensacola, where our unit was headquartered, preparing to leave for overseas. I was on a temporary duty assignment (TDA) to Eglin Air Force Base, special operation headquarters, taking a five-day course.

On the last day of classes, I got word that the unit's battle roster had been changed yet again. This time, however, Danny was on it. This was a member of my section who had been reassigned to an extremely high-risk duty without my knowledge or approval.

When I heard about it, I flew hot. I was as angry as I can ever remember being.

As soon as classes were dismissed, I headed back to our headquarters as fast as I could. During the entire drive I kept going over and over what they had done. They had Danny in a civil affairs team leader slot, assigned to an infantry unit. These teams work on the knife's edge and perform some of the most dangerous jobs in a war zone. Six people to a team, operating without support, out in the red zone, trying to work miracles.

What did they mean taking Danny without even asking me about throwing him into such a slot? I fumed all the way to Pensacola. When I got there, I was almost running across the parking lot to the front door. But as I snatched the door open, the cool air of reality hit me like a sledgehammer.

Danny was the best one to run such a team. It occurred to me that if he were my own son I would have made that same decision, and if my son was on that team I'd be very thankful Danny was leading it. I knew Danny would be a great civil affairs operation team chief. He would field a good team and do the job well. They had made a good decision.

My temperature dropped to normal as I walked in the door. I asked how everything was going and let on like I just stopped by to get a rundown. I never said a word about the changes.

After a month or two in the Iraqi theater of operations, all of us had settled into our jobs. Danny was running the civil affairs team. I was chief of intelligence and senior field advisor to the Iraqi Ministry of Agriculture.

When I was back in the green zone, I liked to watch the teams come and go in and out of the gates. Sometimes I would see them operating in the red zones. It was like watching a movie, except this was real, and we were in it.

The civil affairs advisors and teams had front-row seats, with major roles to play, making history as we did. We interacted with the Iraqi and coalition powers on a daily basis. It was dangerous work sometimes, but very rewarding all the time. No matter what our government's agenda is or was, or whether its decisions were good or bad, the American soldier was there with the noblest of reasons. As always, we were there to help the United States assist these people in a win, to do what's right, and to be good representatives of our country.

Close to the end of our year in Iraq, I was bursting with pride at the way our teams conducted themselves. They were professional, courageous, and smart. They accepted the hardships and did their best every day.

I have made this statement many, many times and have written it before: I would give anything if every American citizen could have ridden with Danny or one of the other teams on one of their missions.

Looking past the element of fear, one would see unbelievable professionalism, courage, and confidence that the United States was doing right by leading and setting good examples. One would never doubt that our kids have what it takes. One would feel the pride and see the real heart of the United States.

And they would be changed forever.

Danny's team did great things in Iraq. He was a great leader as well as a role model and a goodwill ambassador for the United States.

I know Danny went on several more deployments after Iraq—to places like Haiti and South America—and I always heard good things about what he was doing. Since then, he retired as a light colonel, bringing an honorable conclusion to a brilliant career.

He's now a successful businessman who has been elected to serve his community as a school board member.

Danny also has a beautiful family—a family who suffered a tremendous blow when he lost his lovely and loving wife many years too early. But I know that despite their heartache Danny and the kids will honor and keep her memory alive forever.

Danny and his family are a great example of what I believe is best about our country: Duty, honor, country. Godspeed, Danny. Keep setting that example for others. We are all very proud of you, and we are better people for having you in our lives.

Grandmother Nellie, Uncle Willie, and Family Influences on My Early Life

T HINKING OF MY GRANDMOTHER ON MY MOTHER'S SIDE, Nellie Smith, brings back pleasant memories. She pretty much set me in my ways as a country boy and encouraged my quest for adventure, building things, and dreaming.

Grandma Nellie was an unassuming countrywoman in her sixties, or that is the age I first remember her. My dad, mother, and brother, Salari, and I lived on the old homeplace for the first nine years of my life. I think grandma and her brother, Uncle Willie, and his boys and family made a big impression on me. I learned the southern and country ways, and my lifestyle evolved and has been based on what I learned and dreamed of in those early years.

Grandma Nellie always had long, uncut hair, swept up in a bun, hairnet, or bonnet. Long, uncut hair had something to do with her religion and upbringing. She always wore an apron, and was always canning, cooking, cleaning, working in the yard, or going to church, but she always had time to answer my questions and tell me the Lord wouldn't like me doing such and such. During these times I was a straight-A student and would have never made anything less had we stayed in the country in the environment I loved. My peer group was wholesome, maybe a little naive about worldly things, but purely all Americana and certainly American Rockwell based.

One of Grandma's pet talks I'll always remember was about the proper way of shaking hands, and I passed it down to my children.

Handshakes have been around since the birth of civilization. In fact, I think they were initially a way to prove one had no weapons in their hand when meeting someone new. Given today's state of affairs, that might not be a bad idea. Nowadays we use handshakes in meetings, greetings, offering congratulations, closing a business deal, or sometimes to say, "How's it going?" So shake hands firmly and look people in the eye.

Whatever the reason for a handshake, it should become part of a person's repertoire. Handshakes are a sign of trust and to build a personal image. Imagine meeting a well-groomed, well-dressed person for the first time, but they offer a weak handshake. This might create an unfavorable first impression. People are more likely to overlook some visible flaws than a weak handshake. The inverse is true as well.

My sons grew up learning to shake hands. We shook hands a lot; they probably got tired of me telling them about Grandma's handshaking philosophy. But I'm proud of their handshakes. Thanks, Grandma.

Uncle Willie (Little Willie) was about five feet tall, but a giant in my eyes. He always wore overalls and was the spirit and life of all get-togethers. He and his family of eight kids owned and lived on the forty acres in an old early American cracker-type house, behind Grandma Nellie's forty acres. His family, looking back, had very limited resources, but I never realized that back then. They were always busy, working, playing, and enjoying life. They always had food on the table and a grand family atmosphere, even if there were three to the bed sometimes.

I can still remember the way their house smelled of fresh cooking, old clean washed wood floors, and smokey oak and lightered flavors wafting from the fireplace. Their chicken yard was almost as big as

Grandma's, and it had a plum orchard in it. The hog kettle was under the large live oak in the side yard. Willie's boys were my mentors and heroes growing up. They all were larger than life to me.

There were Lonzie (Alonzo), James, Carey, Martha Dell, and Joe, who I didn't know very well, but I knew of them and saw them when they came home for visits. Then there were Morgan, Fain, Violet, and Jimmy. They were my favorites. Morgan was so cool, the Fonzie, the young Elvis of our community. Morgan was talented, handsome, and had a great outgoing personality. He was our local hero and protector. Morgan was actually named after him.

Fain was older than some of the other boys and had a learning disability, but he was one of us. And we all took care of Fain when he wasn't watching after us. The oldest child was Martha Dell, and Violet was the youngest.

Jimmy was about my age, and I was closer to Jimmy than the other boys. We hung out together, played, and worked in the fields. Morgan, his brother, and Jimmy were in Vietnam at the same time. Jimmy was an Airborne trooper and was killed in action. All the boys in the Sexton family served in the military, except Fain. I've thought about Jimmy often; he and his family suffered a great loss. Jimmy's death was deeply moving and had a significant influence on me.

Growing up, we boys all went to the wash hole, the best swimming place in Graves Creek due to its tree cable and homemade diving board. Jimmy, Wayne Redd, and I built tree houses everywhere we could when we could find the lumber. In our minds, we owned the hill and the creek bottom.

We had the best childhood. We had heroes, friends, and role models. We didn't have a care in the world, until the fifth grade. Then things went a little south.

My family and I moved to town. That was the end of my storybook life—new peer group and no more outdoor adventures, or at least not many. My grades and attitude went down and never came back to full trot until after graduation from the Army Rangers in 1973.

Years of average grades, less than great motivation, and subconscious bitterness enveloped me. I was just passing the time, with no outstanding development, living an exceedingly ordinary existence. There were only a few highlights and great times, most of which came during the summer back in the country at Grandma's. My naivety went away. There wasn't a Norman Rockwell world, except for the the summers and the times I was back in the country.

How I Remember My Dad

I N 2011 MY DAD, BUSTER BROWNIE (BB), PASSED AWAY AT eighty-six years old. He was born on January 6, 1924, and his given name was Ben William Franklin Barbee.

I remember the first horse my dad got me, but I can't remember his name. I had to climb a fence to throw the saddle on his back. It took me forever to saddle him up. Four of us kids could ride him at a time—that is, until the meanest young man threw a rock at his rear end, and the horse threw us all.

I remember the first gun dad gave me, a .410 single shotgun. I spent many an hour cleaning and wiping it down with oil. I even sat there on the floor with it while cleaning it and oiling it, checking it out, cocking and uncocking it for practice, as dad showed me. He said I might pull the hammer back and then still shoot it, so I had to learn how to cock it by holding the hammer and pulling the trigger and letting the hammer down easy. It was like Christmas again every time I cleaned and practiced uncocking it.

I remember mother telling me that dad had been at Pearl Harbor, wherever that was, when the Japanese bombed it. She told me that dad was only seventeen when he was there. I remember growing up, knowing he was present at a historical event. I was proud of that.

I remember visiting him at the City of Blountstown's power plant, which furnished electricity to the town for many years after World War II. Dad was the superintendent of the plant. It was an intimidating, big, loud, scary, industrialized type of place. The plant had several World War II–era liberty ship diesel engines that ran all the time. The cement floor was always cold. The plant was always a little scary to be in, but my dad was there with me, so it was okay. I was safe.

I remember the first deer I shot. I even remember the first squirrel I shot with that .410 shotgun. Dad was with me at each event. I remember him teaching me how to clean the game as a little feller.

I remember dad coming back to camp later than the rest of us after a morning hunt, with his bag limit of squirrel, ducks, a turkey, and a deer. He did that twice, and I have never heard or seen anyone else do that. I just grinned as the other kids and I cleaned and dressed the squirrels and ducks.

I remember growing up, and even in adulthood, always seeing dad with a bag of iced-down oysters. I believed he must have eaten oysters every day during the season.

I remember dad being a good cook. He loved the outdoors, hunting and fishing, and camp cooking.

I remember the things dad taught me growing up. He was a no-nonsense instructor. I could wire and plumb a house while still in high school. I also could build a barn or a shed or a camp house. These are skills I have remembered, and they have served me well. I have built many houses, barns, sheds, and camps over the years.

My mama told me a story about when dad was wiring an electrical box for the church across from the house. She was holding me in her arms, watching dad work, as I was still an infant. While we were standing there, in came a feller named Stub Franklin, and he said, "Let me hold that baby."

Mama said she let him hold me, as he watched dad wire the first and largest electrical box, a two-hundred-amp box, in the county at the time. Stub Franklin said, "Brownie, when you get that box wired, I'm calling you an electrician."

I remember me driving him, Carl Bryant, and another man to Jacksonville to join the merchant marines. I had already been off in the merchant marines and was a card-carrying AFL-CIO-SIU Union man at eighteen years old, with a merchant seaman's documents and card. I had come home from the merchant marines and was drafted into the US Army, and I was home on leave. Dad and the other fellow were in their fifties. They were going to see "Tony," the port union hall director, to try to buy—bribe—their way into the union. I don't know if his name was Tony or not, but I told everyone the merchant marines and the union were run by the Italian Mafia, and all port directors were named "Tony."

When we got to the union hall in Jacksonville, there I met this "Tony." I had never tried to bribe anyone before and didn't know where to start, so I said to Tony, while clearing my throat and hesitating, "Sir, what does it take … to get my dad and two other fellows into the merchant marines and the union?"

We were in a back room, and Tony just looked at me for a long moment. Then he said, "Where are these guys located?"

I motioned outside as I said, "Out front in the lobby."

Tony said, "Come over here and show me your dad." We walked over to a window, and I pointed out dad. Tony looked at him, then looked back at me and said, "You go back outside and send them in here to see me."

I waited for almost an hour. There were men sitting all around the union hall, waiting for ships, I guess. Finally, dad, Carl, and the unnamed man came out. I asked how it went. All dad said was, "Let's go and get out of here." We all went down to get their pictures taken and some papers filled out, and before the day was out dad and the others were merchant seamen. I think I was right. The unions were controlled by the mob. Dad never did tell me what happened or how much it cost. Dad sailed as a master electrician for several years, until he grew tired of it. Dad was already retired from the state, so I think he was just doing this for fun, travel, and excitement.

One thing I know, dad never sat in a union hall waiting on a ship. "Tony" always called him at home and asked him if he wanted a ship going to such and such place.

Note: We both received Vietnam service medals for serving in Vietnam with the merchant marines. I still haven't bribed anyone, but I think dad, Carl, and the unnamed man might have.

I remember many a day sitting in the Nettle Ridge Freewill Southern Baptist Church's main auditorium, glancing up at the ceiling during services to see my dad's handprint on the ceiling tile. He had left his mark as he helped hang fixtures for the new church. I looked up at it many a time wondering how someone had hung that light so high up there. I looked at it for a good fifteen to eighteen years and wondered if the print was still there. I must stop by to see if the church has ever changed the lights and the ceiling tiles.

I remember dad as being larger than life, and when he said something I listened. I remember dad always taking his change out of his pocket and giving it to me. He always said, "Here, take this. Young boys always need a little money in their pocket."

I can't remember anything that dad could not do.

I remember him telling me when I got my military commission as an officer, "Always remember, son, who runs the military—your NCOs. You take care of them, back them up, and they will train you, then you will be a better officer."

I remember what someone told me that dad said after I was drafted during the Vietnam conflict. They said they asked him how he felt about me being drafted and going off to war. He said, "If I could go in his place, I would, but it's his turn." That was my dad.

I remember my first deer.

I remember him building our first pole barn. I was about seven or eight years old. It was built out of real cypress poles harvested from the river swamp. The logs were the size of telephone poles. That barn is still standing. My first horse was housed in that barn, along with his feed and tack. I loved playing in that barn. The Sexton boys used to have barn dances in it. I wasn't allowed to attend, as I was too young, but I listened in and watched from a distance.

I remember when dad would let me go to the auction barn in Blountstown, when there was no auction, and no one was there. We would take the dogs, and he would throw them into the cattle vat trough behind the auction barn. The dogs would swim out and go load up in the truck. The purpose of the drenching was to get rid of any insects they might have been carrying. I was so little. Throwing the dogs in seemed cruel, but dad said he was doing them a favor, so all seemed okay.

Dad, the boys, and I were invited down to the Eglin field naval base in Panhandle Florida. The military was going to present a medal to the Pearl Harbor survivors from Florida who were still living. His only surviving son and his grandkids got to witness the ceremony and see him presented with that medal. It was a proud and memorable day for us, but dad seemed in his own thoughts and didn't say much. It seemed like a sad day for him in a way, but us being with him on that day made it a great day. I'm so glad the boys were there. Dad never talked about the war or the Pearl Harbor attack.

On his deathbed, Bonita held his hand and talked with him. She told Brownie that he didn't have to worry about me; she would take care of me. Brownie smiled, winked at her, shut his eyes, and passed away. That was my dad. He was a good dad and grandpa.

Remembering my mom will be published in a later publication, Special Mom.

Remembering Brandon

B RANDON WAS UNIQUE, AS ALL CHILDREN ARE. I GREATLY miss him, although he is with me every day. He even went to Iraq with me and walked and talked with me. Brandon passed away on January 15, 2003, due to a terrible accident in Troy, Alabama, where he was enrolled in college. He was majoring in criminology and was in the ROTC program at Troy State University. Brandon was also on the college rodeo team. He was a bull rider and helped organize and provide leadership for the team.

Brandon loved and was loved by his family and all who knew him. Brandon carried himself like no one I had ever seen before, even though he was my son, and I'm biased. Brandon had a likable, high-standard way about himself. He was not threatening nor heavy-handed and did not provoke resentment. Brandon was a leader and a role model for others. He liked everyone and projected a sense of love and care for others, and it showed through his everyday activities. I personally don't think he knew how he was perceived by his peers and even adults. He was just a genuine southern-mannered young man with an awesome, pleasing personality. I was a proud dad.

I remember Brandon in so many ways and related to so many stories, but I can only share a few here.

James "Jim" Barbee and Brandon were brothers and great buddies. Brandon was so proud of Jim, and he protected and watched over him. Brandon took Jim with him everywhere, and Jim knew great love and was devoted to and admired Brandon. They were bonded together forever. They had a great relationship, even with the six-year difference in age. They never embarrassed one another; they were a pair. They would do anything for each other. Brandon provided good leadership for Jim, and Jim responded to that training Brandon gave him. Their relationship was special and inspiring.

Matthew, Brandon's and Jim's older brother, was more academic and not so much an outdoor person. Matthew was serious about his education, and his interests were different. Brandon and Jim were proud of him and would go to war for Matthew, and Matthew for them. They all shared a great love for each other.

Bow hunting and bow fishing were hobbies that Brandon dearly enjoyed, and he shared his interests not only with his brother Jim but with his friends as well. Brandon learned to weld aluminum while we were building the platforms for the bow fishing boat. I bet half of the kids in Brandon's class and dozens of others went with us at one time or another on that boat. Brandon and Jim never missed an opportunity to go. We all spent many an hour enjoying those experiences.

Bull riding was another passion that Brandon had cultivated. How he got the idea to want to ride a bull, I don't know, but he stayed after me to help find a place where he could go and learn the ways of bull riding. After several reminders and thoughts about all the consequences, I relented. I wasn't going to stand in the way of something he wanted to do that badly. I heard about the practice pens at a Mr. Grady Harper's up in Georgia, near Colquitt. So we made arrangements to go there one Sunday afternoon.

Brandon was hooked more than ever after visiting Mr. Harper's farm and bull-riding pens. Over the next two years or so, we spent many a Sunday up there riding bulls, or at least trying to. There was great fellowship to be had in the new adventure. Jim and Brandon made many new friends, and several young people from Calhoun

County made it to those afternoon practices. It seemed like half of Blountstown High began wearing cowboy hats. Many got on their first-ever bulls there at Mr. Grady's practice pens in Hentown, Georgia.

Brandon went on to join the Southern Professional Bull Riders Association (SPBR) and was runner-up rookie of the year that first year, when he was about seventeen years old. He won a little money at several different rodeos, and he enjoyed himself. Brandon also joined the Alabama High School Rodeo Association because no school in North Florida had a rodeo team. He actually was able to letter in rodeoing at Blountstown High School and wore that patch proudly on his letterman jacket. Jim and I tagged along, me watching and Jim riding the young bulls. Jim was quite the rider himself. Between Brandon and Jim, they had been on a hundred or so bulls within the first few years. I just grinned, worried, and hoped for the best.

On Brandon's eighteenth birthday, Jim and I rode our first big bulls. Jim had been riding since he was twelve years old—the smaller young bulls—but that day he rode one of the big ones. Brandon was there for us both. It's amazing what folks do out of peer pressure and love. Jim and I were carried along by the excitement, zeal, and passion with which Brandon lit our world.

Brandon went on to enroll at Troy State University after graduating from Chipola College. Troy was starting a rodeo team, one of the first in the Southeast, and Brandon became a collegiate bull rider and helped to develop Troy State's first rodeo team.

As I watched Brandon growing up, I knew he had something special about him: his looks, his smile, how he carried himself, how he treated and genuinely cared for others. He didn't meet many strangers and had a great handshake and introduction. He didn't know it, but he was well liked and looked up to by his peers and many younger kids. Even the adults took notice of his conduct and demeanor. Brandon became a role model for many younger kids. We were very proud of how he handled the fanfare. If he even realized he had that way about himself, I don't know. I don't think he understood how he was seen by others. He was just a super friendly, caring, happy, thoughtful, giving kind of fellow. It was hard not to like Brandon.

The same year that Brandon passed, 2003, I deployed to Iraq. I didn't and still don't know how to grieve; I just could not accept Brandon was gone. I, as well as the entire family, had a difficult time believing he was gone. Every step I took in Iraq, Brandon was with me. I almost didn't want to come home, as I knew he wouldn't be there.

We all miss Brandon so much. He had much to offer.

I love my boys. They are all different, in their own ways, and I'm proud of them.

Godspeed.

Remembering Jimmy Clyde Sexton: Friend, Cousin, Good Buddy—Killed in Action, Vietnam

I MISS JIMMY AND THINK OF HIM AND HIS FAMILY OFTEN. I'M
a better person because of the memories of their family and
the country ways in which we were raised. Jimmy's entire family was
amazing to me. They were rich in life, in ways I think about often.
Living in the rural South had its challenges and hardships, but the
Sextons were some of the finest folk I have ever known.

The Sextons lived on a back rural forty acres that they owned
and farmed. It was a pleasure and an adventure every time I visited
with them. I was closest in age to Jimmy Clyde, and we shared more
time together in our early youth. His older brother, Morgan Sexton,
was sort of our hero. There wasn't anything Morgan couldn't do.
When Jimmy was killed in Vietnam, Morgan was over there in
and around Vietnam at the same time. The day of Jimmy's burial
was an unbelievable day in my life. His family asked if I could be a
pallbearer; I could *not* do it. It was more than I could take at that
time. I didn't believe that could be Jimmy—not alive? I truly hope the
family understood. I had never cried so hard. I wasn't strong enough
to handle that loss; I think I was sixteen that year. Three years later
I was drafted and went willingly. I miss and still think about Jimmy
and his family—a lot. Godspeed, Jimmy and family. I've tried to live

up to what I saw growing up with y'all and watching how y'all tackled the world. Thank you for the great influences. I bet y'all didn't even know how your lives influenced others. Love y'all.

Rest in peace, Jimmy ole buddy.

THE ENGAGEMENT IN WHICH JIMMY WAS KILLED

O PERATION MASHER/WHITE WING WAS THE FIRST Cavalry Division's name for their part of an allied operation conducted against main force Vietcong (VC) and North Vietnamese Army (NVA) units operating in southeastern Quang Ngai Province and northeastern Binh Dinh Province. The combined VC-NVA force was the Sao Vang (Gold Star) Division—a force totaling nearly three divisions of US Army, US Marines, Korean army, and South Vietnamese army—were staged against them.

The allied sweep of the operation area began on January 24, 1966, and continued for six weeks, officially ending on March 6. The First Cavalry Division mounted out its First and Third Brigades. By mid-February, the cavalry had operated from the coastal areas into the interior mountains. Based on intelligence data that the Second VC Regiment was concentrated in the hills south and east of the Kim Son Valley, the focus of the First Cavalry Division's offensive changed. On February 17, the Fifth Cavalry caught the heavy weapons battalion of the Second VC Regiment, leading to a series of engagements over the next several days.

On February 23, the First Battalion, Twelfth Cavalry, lost twenty men in an especially hard-fought engagement:

A Company
* SSG Matthew Hough, Bethune, South Carolina
* SSG Marshall R. Smith, Lakewood, California

- SGT Charles R. Dale, Gaithersburg, Maryland
- SGT Charles E. Dyson, Philadelphia, Pennsylvania
- SGT Paul J. Stochaj, Webster, Massachusetts
- SP4 Joe N. James, Oakland, California
- SP4 Richard Rangel, San Bernardino, California
- SP4 Frankie Sanchez, Dodge City, Kansas
- PFC William H. Coburn, Chesapeake, Virginia
- PFC Jimmy C. Sexton, Blountstown, Florida
- PVT Winston Morris, Chicago, Illinois

B Company
- 2LT Donald B. Adamson, Grand Rapids, Michigan
- SGT Patrick C. Nevin, East Chicago, Indiana

C Company
- SFC Dalmer D. Jurek, Caldwell, Texas
- PFC Isaiah Mulwee, Bridgeport, Connecticut
- PFC Tommy L. Nicholas, Decatur, Alabama
- PFC Kenneth A. Reynolds, Washington, DC
- PFC Marvin J. Wilson, Crosby, Minnesota

HQ Company
- SSG William B. Watson, Durham, North Carolina PFC Dove El Hondah, Chicago, Illinois

THE DOCTOR I CALLED
SLOW LEAK

I T WAS A CHILLY, RAINY DAY IN SARAJEVO, IN THE FORMER Yugoslavia, during 1997.

"Doc," I said, "you wouldn't give that SOB a ride if it was raining like this, would you?"

Slow Leak, a nickname I called the doc from time to time, answered, "Hell no, I wouldn't give that bastard a ride or anything else."

Little did Slow Leak know, he had been set up. Despite that predictable answer, I knew this gruff Yankee from New York had another side, and I'm about to tell it—I already had a photo of him giving the guy a ride on a rainy day from a month earlier.

The Christmas Party

W E MET AT A CHRISTMAS PARTY ON A COLD, GLOOMY night in that foreign land known as Bosnia and Herzegovina. Most of our task force of several hundred special operations soldiers with the 350th Civil Affairs Command had been through one heck of a deployment, with long hours and little guidance or direction from our command.

To this point, we had been engaged mainly in meaningless activities that required long hours of made-up work and lots of hurry-up-and-wait. Nowhere could I see that we were contributing to the US mission and helping the Croats, Bosnians, or Serbs in this war-torn land.

We had been in-country about two months, and we would be spending Christmas in-country. Morale was way down, and our stress levels were way up. Most of the task force lived in a place called the residence. It was a building that had been occupied by at least five occupying armies and sat within eyesight of the bridge where Archduke Ferdinand of Austria-Hungary was assassinated, setting off the First World War.

Given the gloomy weather and ominous surroundings, combined with the sour mood of the troops, I decided what we needed was a Christmas party. It was quite the affair. We had taken over the second story of the building, and our soldiers and some from other units started filing in. My section, the 2-shop, were taking donations to fund beverages for lowering the inhibitions of personnel.

After about an hour, all was going well, and we were enjoying great fellowship. It was clear that everyone had been needing and looking forward to this break in the otherwise dreary work. While I was standing next to the beverage table, LTC Michael Canale, a doctor and medical officer, walked up and asked who was putting on this event. Everyone close by pointed to the wall sign that read the 2-shop was sponsoring the activity and hoped everyone would have a Merry Christmas and a good time.

Doc Canale handily said he would like to help sponsor the occasion and handed over about twenty dollars. So I took my magic marker and edited the sign so that it now read "Sponsored by the 2-Shop and the Medical Section."

That was my first formal introduction to Dr. Michael Canale. About forty minutes later, I witnessed this same medical professional, our command doctor, running down the hall with a beer in one hand, soaking wet, yelling, then dropping and sliding headfirst down the beer-soaked hall floor. Doc was sliding toward and between the legs of a young woman who had positioned herself as a target at the other end of the hall. Apparently, this was the object of the game.

I was probably the only sober one on the second floor at this time, and all I could think about was the "tailhook" party that landed a bunch of navy officers in hot water. But the troops needed a little loosening up and some celebrating, and Doc was leading the way. Besides, things seemed well under control.

But that didn't last long.

The first time the MPs came up to the second floor, they seemed okay and were even in good holiday spirits. They asked if we could hold it down just a little. The soldiers complied, showed respect, and briefly pulled themselves together.

In what seemed like the blink of an eye, however, I saw some soldiers pick up the five-gallon water cooler jug off the dispenser and pour it up and down the hall to help with the sliding.

While this was going on, soldiers on both sides of the hall were pouring beer into the mix. It was almost ankle-deep, and the stairs looked like a waterfall. That's when the MPs arrived the second time. They had lost their Christmas spirit on this visit and highly recommended we break up the second-floor party.

I stepped in and let everyone know it was time to straighten up, clean up, and spread out, maybe down to the cellar bar and lounge area. To their credit, the troops quickly sorted themselves out and made their way to their quarters or to a quieter party elsewhere. I was grateful that we'd been able to have a good party without anything getting too out of hand.

The party was still on my mind the next morning at the command briefing. I had been thinking that some of the previous night's activities might be frowned upon by the command and that something might come up later. I decided to be proactive and speak to our commander after the briefing. As I did so, I noticed Doc Canale settled nearby, paying close attention to me.

I told the commander we had a little party over at the residence, and everyone seemed to enjoy it. I told him I didn't see anyone getting way out of hand, but if anything came up I wanted him to know I was the person in charge. The commander just said he'd heard it was a "helluva party" and that he was glad the soldiers had a good time.

When the commander left, Doc and I were the only ones left in the briefing room. He approached me, and I wasn't sure what he was going to say. I was a little surprised when he shook my hand and said, "Barbee, I like you. You're a stand-up guy."

Looking back, I think he might have been a little concerned I was going to go into detail about the party and start naming names or try to blame someone else. When I didn't, Slow Leak realized I might be all right.

That was my first real introduction to Doc Canale. I still didn't know him well, but I was about to learn. What I learned was that to say Slow Leak was a little different would be very much an understatement.

Doc wasn't from around where I grew up, and that in itself made me a little leery. Plus, he was a Yankee from New York City, for God's sake. But he did have a quality that I admire in some folks. He was sneaky and devious, and since I spend time watching folks and trying to learn things he was ripe for my observations. I found myself entertained by his antics and his ways of addressing situations.

I decided I could learn something from this Yankee.

A Collector of Characters

D oc Canale really was a qualified medical doctor, but I always kidded him, saying, "He probably graduated in the lower half of his class." That's because he was very seldom a serious-acting doctor. Most of the time he also seemed pissed off—at people, races, cultures, life, and even God.

Slow Leak was definitely a different kind of doctor, but down deep—and I do mean deep—he really cared about some of the same things I cared about, specifically our troops and the United States.

He was also borderline psychotic. I say that because he hung out with and bunked with the strangest soldiers from several different armies: ours, the French, the Italians, and others. It was like he was studying them.

The foreign soldiers all seemed a little offbeat to me, but it was like he was their savior. He watched after them most of the time and made fun of them the rest. Make note, no one else could pick at them in front of him. Together they were a sight to behold. I referred to them all as the oddballs, but only to Slow Leak.

He must have minored in psychology or psychiatry or some other shrink stuff because he analyzed everyone and every situation. It was hilarious to watch him and listen to him talk about various people and his assessment of them.

Slow Leak and I got along great, by the way. In fact, I was one of the few officers who he could even tolerate, much less trust or confide in. No matter what kind of a front he put up, he knew I had his number.

For example, I was there one day when he received word a soldier had been hurt. As much as he seemed to dislike people, Doc took off on foot several miles across town to get to him. He cared very deeply; he just didn't want anyone to know.

The Map and the Making of an Intelligence Operator

A S THE INTELLIGENCE OPERATIONS OFFICER AND CHIEF OF intelligence for the task force, I was responsible for clearances, daily intelligence briefings, and something else that had never been done within the civil affairs community. It was something we call passive intelligence, or passive information gathering.

For this yearlong mission, I set up a passive information system. My goal was to get as many of our field operators as possible to collect and report all the information they gathered or ran across and to inform me of things they worked on in their day-to-day operations.

By our charter, civil affairs units do not gather intelligence on the host countries where we work. We did not want to break any trust or spoil any goodwill that we might build in working with the locals, national military, or local governments. The civil affairs community is fairly well indoctrinated in this concept, and it was difficult for our commander and our operators to accept even this limited intelligence role.

But the fact is, there were almost no CIA or State Department operators in the country—only one of each. By contrast, civil affairs had people placed in every strategic position within the country. We had a unique opportunity but would have to change some of our concepts in order to collect valuable information.

This may have been the first time in combat operations in which a civil affairs task force deployed with an intelligence operations section and actively managed a passive information mission. I even received a pretty significant military commendation for the intel operation we ran.

I give credit to the soldiers and officers who understood what we were trying to do and worked hard to help. But, as always, there were a few who were slow to either understand the program or buy into it.

Slow Leak was in the latter group. Doc said he didn't think there was anything he was exposed to that would be worthwhile. I knew that wasn't true, however, so I asked him offhandedly if he ever saw any maps in the places he worked.

It turns out there was a great map that everyone looked at and referenced right in the foyer of his office. It identified and labeled all the hospitals, clinics, and other medical facilities in Bosnia. I thought to myself, *Now that would be an incredibly important document to some intel analyst.*

I asked Doc if he might be able to get a copy, but he balked and said that would be difficult because the map was in a frame. But he promised he would try.

Time passed, and Slow Leak was my only nonproducer. Everybody else had gotten me something. I kept asking, but even after several weeks I still had nothing from him.

Among Doc's many other talents, he was a great ass-kisser. As such, he managed to wangle a trip with our commander around Europe for a few days. With him on such an important mission, I figured the least I could do would be to help him out with the map.

I recruited another solider, and the two of us went over to where Doc worked.

We asked if he was in, even though we knew he wasn't, and when told he was out we asked to leave a note on his desk. On the way out the door, I stopped and admired the big map in the entryway. I complimented Doc's staff on having such a nice, helpful guide to all the country's medical facilities. Then I asked, incidentally, if they might need more maps for their other locations. I explained we had access to large printers and would be happy to make them copies.

"Sure," came the response from everyone within earshot, and within a few minutes the other soldier and I had the map out of the frame and headed back to the 2-shop.

The day after Slow Leak returned from his European junket, he showed up in my office with a "go-to-hell" look on his face.

"Barbee, how in the hell did you do that?" he asked.

"Do what?"

"You know damn well what I'm talking about," he said. "There were maps taped all over my wall in the office, one on the conference table, and one draped over my desk. I could hardly get into my office there were so many maps, and every one of the Bosnian medical staff had copies as well."

The original was back in its place in the lobby, and despite his initial reluctance Slow Leak Canele became one of my best information gatherers. That might have had something to do with the fact that the map was a big hit at the Pentagon, in Molesworth, England, and with some three-letter agencies.

Of course, I gave Doc great credit and praise for uncovering his hidden "intel" talents. He was a good collections operator and a better man for the experience. Working outside his field and contributing in different ways improved his attitude considerably. He would go on to become one of the heroes of Bosnia before we left.

THE JOKE

Doc Canale did have a sense of humor, although I certainly didn't think so at first. He seemed a little slow on the uptake, thus the nickname, and didn't smile or laugh a lot. Truthfully, I was a little worried that his mannerisms—and occasional lack of manners—might put off some folks, especially since he worked around a sea of southerners.

In hindsight, I realize he was probably a little suspicious of me because I was suspicious of him. And that's because I always felt like he was guilty of something that he just hadn't been caught doing quite yet.

Still, I remember the exact day and circumstance in which I finally gained his trust, and he relaxed a little. We were riding out to the other side of Sarajevo, near a place called Daisy World. Being from New York, Doc was hard on people, too hard at times. It struck me that maybe he just needed to loosen up a bit.

As he was driving, I was busy shredding a white napkin into tiny delicate shreds and carefully hiding the pieces in one hand.

I don't always tell off-color jokes, but I felt like in this situation it would serve a greater good. I also can't repeat it in this writing, but I'll describe it.

After I had finished tearing up the napkin, I asked Doc a question that involved … let's just say intimate relations and a chicken.

Without going into too much detail, the punch line was simply me coughing into the hand holding the shredded napkin pieces, blowing them all over the Humvee's interior.

I don't know how many people would find that joke funny, but at that moment there was nobody in Europe laughing harder than Dr. Michael Canele. He laughed so hard in fact that we veered off the road and across the railroad tracks. When we came to a stop, Doc was hanging out of the vehicle, head down, and still laughing as hard as I had ever seen anyone, anywhere.

I reached over and pushed the red button on his seat belt, and Doc tumbled to the ground, still laughing. That's when I saw the Spanish MPs heading our way, wondering what in the heck was going on. I don't know what Doc told them after he stopped laughing, but it worked. They went their way, and we went ours.

A little ways down the road, Doc looked over at me and said, "Don't ever do something like that to me again."

He might deny it, but I overheard him telling that joke several times while we were in Sarajevo, and I found bits of shredded napkins all over the compound.

I had my doubts about Slow Leak in the beginning. I thought he might be crazy. In the end, I learned to like him because he was crazy.

Note: He's a good friend of mine to this day. Imagine if I didn't like him!

How Do I Explain
That Feeling?

A S OF LATE, I'VE BEEN PUTTING A FEW RANDOM THOUGHTS down on paper. I've been writing about my military service years, about my boys, about my teaching years, hunting, fishing, a little about many things. In my research, I ran across a paper that Jim, one of my youngest sons, wrote many years ago when he was around fifteen or sixteen. He wanted to enter an essay contest that the National Turkey Federation was sponsoring.

Jim came to me and asked, "Dad, how do you explain to someone who doesn't hunt what it feels like when you hear that first big gobbler sound off early in the morning?"

Well, needless to say, that was a difficult question that caught me off guard, as usual. I gave him an answer after a bit of thinking, then I forgot about it. I want to share the little letter he wrote that year, and even though he didn't win in the eyes of the Turkey Federation, he won in my mind. He must be winning still. Every time I try to get up with him, he's gone hunting. It ain't a bad way to live.

HOW CAN YOU EXPLAIN
THAT FEELING?

By Jim Barbee, Age Sixteen

Y NAME IS JIM BARBEE, AND I WAS BORN AND LIVE IN A small town between two rivers in North Florida, and as long as I can remember, I have been a hunter.

A family friend used to come to our house when I was younger. She would always come over and say, "Hello, Jungle Jim." I'm seventeen now, and she still calls me Jungle Jim. Every time she came into our yard, she saw me with a bow, knives, bullwhips, or some other type of hunting device in my hands. At least she thinks of me as a hunter.

My brother and I always used to wait for hunting season all year. It would be forever coming. We practiced and prepared for hunting year-round. My fondest memories and the most significant advantage that I've had in my life is the love of my brothers and father. They showed me the joys of working and playing hard. My appreciation of the outdoors and hunting has been due to their sharing and helping me develop, even when I didn't always understand.

The understanding and the appreciation that I have for the importance of wildlife conservation is an invaluable tool for our future, taught to me by my brother. Brandon once caught and released the largest bass he and I had ever seen. While I did not understand his reasoning, at the time, over the years I was able to see why he made that choice. For him to catch the fish and to have the enjoyment of releasing him was just as important as catching the fish. After years of reflecting on that day, I came to understand. The concept taught to me that day has guided me at times and helps me to understand many things in life.

There is no prettier sight in the world than several big ole gobblers strutting across one of my food plots, early on a foggy cold morning or the feelings inside you when a gobbler, on the roost, cuts loose with a loud gobble at daylight. If there is a more exciting feeling than a gobbler heading your way, gobbling every breath, even after that less than perfect yelp from your mouth call, I haven't yet found it.

I've heard my dad try to explain that feeling to non–turkey hunters before. He said it was something like if you were sitting five seats back, front and center of a grand symphony orchestra as the musicians reached the crescendo. That's when, if you are paying attention, your insides shake. Your diaphragm, separating your ribs, vibrates (needless to say I had to ask him to explain and spell the crescendo part). I've been dragged to several symphonies, and I don't get the same feeling. But come to think about it, how would or could I explain what a large tom, gobbling every breath, heading toward you on a cool, crisp morning, feels like?

My first time with that feeling came when I was only eight years old, and before daylight my dad settled me down between two outcroppings of roots on an old oak tree. As I waited, all my thoughts went into all the things Dad had been telling me about turkey hunting. Sit still, don't move an eyelid, wait till he gets to within twenty yards, let the mosquitoes have their way as the gobbler nears, don't move, make a good head and neck shot. My heart was pumping ninety miles an hour; I could feel my heartbeat in my ears, just a thumping, as the big ten-inch Tom was gobbling, heading my way. I was by myself; Dad was somewhere twenty or so yards behind me, calling. There was no one to turn to, only me to deal with this shaking inside me. The click of the safety, the head comes into view, then a slow move to stay on target. "Boom." Hooked for life.

There isn't any way to capture that feeling or describe it, except being there. So that's where I'll be, come March and April for all the years of my life, in pursuit of Boss Tom.

I hope you'll be able to capture that feeling, one day, if you haven't already, either at a concert, a symphony, or at some event you love.

Jim Barbee, Gone Hunting.

Flinthead Arrows

L ITTLE HISTORICAL NOTE: I BOUGHT A DOZEN RED XX75 aluminum arrows over thirty something years ago and still own three of those arrows. One of them has a flint arrowhead and was made by Mr. Owen House many years ago. I notched that arrow and wrapped, tightened, and glued that flinthead on that arrow. I've killed three deer with that one flinthead arrow and a Howard Hill longbow. I never learned to nap flint very well, but Mr. Owen House perfected it many years ago. The flinthead on that arrow chipped on the first deer kill. I took that flinthead back to Mr. House to get him to try to restore it. He did, and it went back on the arrow. On other arrows, I placed original flintheads I had collected over the years. Flintheads, believe it or not, cut and penetrate well. Only one of my kills wasn't a pass-through. Thanks to Mr. House for his help in making great memories.

Spear Hunting: The Modern-Day Spear Hunter

"**I** could almost touch one, Dad."
This was how it all started in 1999.

One day my middle son, then nineteen-year-old college student Brandon B. Barbee, came up to me and said, "Dad, you wouldn't believe my stand. I have deer coming by so close I can almost touch them."

My first words were, "Where are you hunting?"

"I'm in an old hollow tupelo tree down in a flat."

Well, within the next couple of days, while Brandon was at school, I went looking for his stand. Curiosity had gotten the best of me. He had the perfect ground stand. There it was, in the center of an old dried-up river swamp flat ravine, an ideal open hollow of a river tupelo tree. The opening was a split on one side, with about a five-by-four-foot hollow with a flat leafy bottom. There was one other small opening to the front of the hollow, other than the opening coming into the tree.

Brandon had a folding chair inside and had raked the leaves back from around the tree to expose the soil underneath. He had cleverly placed a pile of corn several feet from the tree. What a beautiful and secluded private place to wait for whitetail deer and wild hogs, with natural camouflage and a scent barrier.

I crawled into the tree and had a seat, and within minutes it seemed like I saw movement to my left. There was my son, heading my way to take his place in the perfect ground stand. Looking at my watch, I realized his school was out for the day, and he was going hunting. Well, I felt a little guilty being caught at his new stand, but he understood, and we talked about him seeing deer coming from the riverside in the evening. I told him what a wonderful place it might be to get a deer with a spear, being that they came in so close. It was just another idea and wasn't taken very seriously at the time, but I couldn't get the idea of possibly hunting deer with a spear out of my mind. It was such an ideal spot.

I have promoted bow hunting and black-powder hunting as a return to the old hunting ways and have mentored others who are like-minded. But the less motivated of us have chosen less-sturdy and less-faithful methods. We have high-teched the archery and black-powder world of hunting too. It's almost like target practice rather than hunting, even with a bow and arrows. But there are still traditionalists out there trying to catch the real hunting feel. We are losing more ground every year because old-fashioned hunting isn't pursued or taught today.

This was the reasoning behind the notion of spear hunting—to try to capture the true art of hunting again. I had to get them involved in the new project, but that wasn't so easy this time. I had to convince them this could be done.

I should have known something was up when both boys seemed to roll their eyes at my new wild project, but their lack of enthusiasm had never stopped me from trying something new. So I pressed on, in my separate world of fancies. Well, it wasn't somewhere I hadn't gone before. After all, while serving in Bosnia with the 361st JTF Special Operations, I started, and we put on the First Bosnia International Invitational Longbow Championship. Also, in Iraq, while serving with the 350th Civil Affairs Special Operation Command, I organized and facilitated the First Iraqi International Invitational

Archery Championship as well as several fishing tournaments for the youth there in Baghdad.

I had even orchestrated three serious rodeos because the boys were engaged in bull riding and other rodeo events. Also, I had started several other at-home projects that the boys scoffed at as well as flatly refused to participate in, like shiitake mushroom production, hog-trap building, houseboat building, and several others projects that they finally warmed up to. They were always telling me to talk to them first before I made any more plans that included them without their approval.

Well, here I went again without their full buy-in to my plans for us. Actually, my middle son, Brandon, was the one who got me started down this road of no return. He had found the best ground blind and agreed that it would make the perfect spearing location, if spear hunting was a thing to do. I chose to follow my idea and assumed everyone would be with me later. Thank you for getting us going down this road, Brandon Barbee.

Back to hunting.

It seems that long ago many of us had gotten the word *hunting* and *shooting* mixed up. Most of today's so-called hunting is done over bait, green patches, and clever attractions, with a smart, convenient, comfortable tree stand overlooking the attractant that we can shoot over. Now don't get me wrong, the excitement is still there for the sightings, the preparations, and the kill, but something has been lost.

To hunt with a spear is crazy and takes it to a whole new level.

First of all, no real hunter, which I sometimes considered myself, would honestly give two thoughts to hunting with a spear. But the Native Americans of old did it, or at least that was what I was always taught. The big question was how do I get that close to a hog or a whitetail deer to place a spear into the kill zone to take them down?

A wild animal is much, much faster than a human. They could detect the movement of the arm and spear much too soon. It may work with a hog, maybe. I have walked up very close to many feral hogs in the wild, but I still didn't think I could ever take one down by stalking and throwing a spear.

Brandon had given me a new perspective on the notion of spear hunting—it could work, as a hollow tree hides scent and movement. But the throwing seemed maybe still out of my skill level, unless I could catch them unaware, which was going to happen.

Next, Brandon and I built two spears to our liking—that is, both were long enough, heavy enough, with a heavy-duty sharp point. It was very seldom that we got something close to correct the first time out, but there still isn't much change I would make, even after all these years.

I had a hollow tree at the other end of one of my food plots in a swampy area. Long before I ever found this place to hunt, loggers had come through and had found this tree that they tested for merchantable timber possibilities. They saw a square hole on one side of the tree about three feet from the ground; the hole was around two-foot by two-foot square. The tree was not merchantable as it was hollow all the way up to the top. The hollow was a good four feet across, with light coming in from the top and the cutout hole. Inside was a leafy, solid dirt and mud floor. Small animals had pretty much cleaned it out, and there were only spiders, webs, and a few other crawling insects that I soon cleared out the best that I could. I placed a folding metal chair inside, and on the outside, I raked back all the leaves, twigs, and driftwood up around the hollow cypress. I turned up some of the fresh dirt—deer seem to like to play or at least sniff around freshly turned dirt. I had gathered up a tub of acorns, crushed them, and spread them around outside the new hollow tree blind.

I spent the next several weeks hunting out of my stand at the other end of the quarter-mile-long food plot. While in my other tree stand, I observed the hollow tree and watched for activity around it. The deer did find the acorns and started hanging out around the base of the hollow. Things were looking up.

For the last two weeks of watching the tree from a distance, I kept thinking, *This is how the Native Americans must have done it. It had to have been.* But I'm sure they had more patience than a modern man. They could hide their scent better, stay still longer, and wait for the animals. Also, instead of throwing the spear like the Native Americans would have, I planned to gig them out of the hollow in the tree.

I knew how to gig frogs and fish, and knew the concept was the same for a larger animal. But gigging a deer would lead to it bolting away as soon as it was hit. That quick take off and jerking was going to throw that spear shaft to one side with a deadly force that could break a jaw, a hand, and or arm. I either had to hold on to the spear very securely or release it very quickly after thrusting forward. What to do, what to do? Once I entered the hollow of that tree, I never continued those thoughts or came up with a satisfactory solution. I sort of forgot about what to do after I gigged the large animal.

The first afternoon I spent three hours in the tree bored to death, thinking about what the heck I was doing; this was crazy and boring. But I did see a couple of deer moving about forty yards from the hollow. I had no idea how many could be outside, either closer or farther away. My whole world was that two-by-two window out the front of the tree. All I could see was what came by that hole in the tree. I did think I heard some activity just outside the tree, but I could not see anything outside the periphery of that hole.

I learned a few things that first afternoon. Spear hunting is a boring and lonely experience, but my excitement and imagination were still flowing.

The next afternoon I took one spear and placed a forked stick up just outside the hole, with a pile of fresh broken open acorns right in front of the stick. I placed the spear back in through the hole high up and rested the spear shaft on the forked stick, with the point positioned about two feet above the acorns. I crawled inside with a book to read.

About two hours later, I started to see activity and movement. Two deer walked by the tree about ten feet in front of the hole, heading up to the plot, but I could sense there were more deer outside looming about. A young doe walked right up to the spear, and her head went down to sniff the acorns. Another doe came up and ate the acorns, with me sitting in the hollow tree not five feet away. The doe looked directly at me for a second or two, and I was frozen in place with both hands holding the book in my lap. Both the doe and fawn moved on. My heart was speeding up—this can happen, and I now know it! There were just sounds behind the tree until dark when I had to get out, and I realized I had just scored them away.

It was a couple of days later before I could go back to the hollow tree. I arrived early with my spear, acorns, and book. I repositioned my spear in the tree and, laying on the forked stick, put out fresh acorns, then climbed back in and had a seat in my folding chair.

While reading in a hollow tree with little very little light except what was mostly coming in the hole, I had to tilt the book forward and hold it out a little to catch enough light to read by. After reading, looking, reading, and looking out through the hole for well over an hour, I nodded off to sleep. I was waking up sometime later with a deer looking at me through the two-foot square hole in the tree. The deer was a young spike buck, and it just kept looking at me at the end of the spear. Every once in a while, he would put his head down and eat in the acorn pile but then shoot his head up to look back into the hollow hole, right at me.

I was still holding the book with both hands and the spear handle with my left shoulder. For well over thirty minutes, the deer kept ducking his head and springing back up to look in at me; all the while I was trying to put the book down to the ground without much movement or noise. The deer was no more than five feet away. We were looking at each other. The only breaks were when he ducked down to get a mouth full of acorns.

After what seemed like two hours, I finally got one hand on the spear and then the other about fifteen minutes later. I was ready, but the young buck was just fidgeting around, and would not move to his side to the spear point. The only shot I had was in the middle back as he ducked his head. I forgot about turning the spear loose when I stuck him or hanging on to it. When I stuck him as hard as I could, I shoved it into the central backbone of his back. He jumped, and the edge of the hole is the only thing that saved me from getting knocked silly with the shaft of the spear. The spear was violently jerked from me, and I never really had a chance to hold on or to turn it loose. It all happened so quickly.

I dove out of the hole in the tree; the spear had pulled out of the deer, leaving his back legs paralyzed. He was running around on his front two legs the best he could, pulling his back legs, which were flopping to and fro. I picked up the spear and was wildly chasing the deer. I made a wild throw of the spear at him as he was running, flopping and moving wildly. I missed, and the spear stuck in the rooty bottom of a bunch of small bushes. As I ran by, I could not pull the spear out, so I kept running after the deer while trying to retrieve my pocketknife from my front pocket. It's impossible to unsheathe a knife while running around bushes, logs, trees, and stumps.

After the deer and I had run about what seemed like a mile, in circles, zigzagging around within one hundred yards of the hollow tree, he flopped once too often. I jumped on him. We were both given out and exhausted, me about to have a heart attack, out of breath, trying to hold down the deer and still trying to retrieve my knife. Both of us seemed in the throes of death. I finally got the knife out, opened it, and tried to cut his throat, while being kicked, catching air, and holding on. Well now, I was learning many valuable lessons on this hunt. It's a wonder I didn't cut myself many, many times trying this technique of hunting. After I thought the deed was done, the fight was just starting. There was more life in the dying deer than there was in me. Blood was going everywhere, feet were pawing and kicking, he was baying like a hurt calf, and I was trying to stick and cut the main veins and slash the neck open more. I had to get this over with. After sufficiently cutting the deer's throat, I was trying to roll away and get back away from the deer, but couldn't. We were both dying.

I was out of breath, sucking wind, heart pumping, totally exhausted. I made one rollover and was trying to catch my breath while the deer was in its last breaths and movements. Both of us were covered in blood. The ground was torn up and looked like there had been a bad knife fight. There were scuff marks, blood, and broken bushes. I'm sure I was pathetic looking. This had been a fight to the death.

I washed and cleaned up the best I could in the nearby creek, after recovering my thinking, about how crazy this hunt was. I sat down by the creek with the deer and spear and contemplated what all had happened. While sitting and collecting my thoughts, I gave thanks for the outcome of this hunt and the many lessons learned. I had to further develop my spear-hunting techniques.

Lessons learned: more patience; aiming point; turn the spear loose, don't keep holding it; have a sharp scabbard knife; and one can be successful spear hunting.

Both Jim and Brandon warmed up to the spear-hunting idea after seeing the results. Sometimes we just have to set the example and plant those learning seeds with a little more patience.

Ambushed

S OME MIGHT WONDER WHAT IT WOULD BE LIKE TO SET UP AN ambush for the business of killing their country's enemies. I trained and practiced many times for doing just that in my US Army training days. We trained on preparations, setting up, initiating, and recovery. My trainers had everything a soldier would need to be successful in different types of ambushes, or so I thought.

They thought of everything, except some of the most important considerations, such as the weather factors as well as psychosocial and psychological differences of soldiers. Ambushes take a toll on the body and mind due to the waiting, initiating, and the aftermath of ambushes. I believe these last factors need to be incorporated into our soldiers' training.

Ranger Nights

It's almost here. Ranger weather. Activity time. There is nothing like the rain dripping from the brim of one's hat late at night while they wait. The flashing of lightning adds to the flavor, engages the senses, and concentrates the mind on the task at hand. When the thunder is rolling in, even better. One will never feel so alive or feel more like a soldier. There is also a lonely factor, but it is coated with a feeling of great satisfaction and determination.

When it's time to move, the heart jumps a little, and the training kicks in, with the steady rhythm of the mind and eyes focusing on the tasks ahead. With initiation, the training continues, and the steady calmness of being successful is clear and demanding. Afterward there is more calmness. The mind is more in play as one contemplates, clarifies, and justifies their actions.

Some will understand. Some will agree. Some will have different thoughts. I'm just thinking out loud as the storm rolls in. Good night. I hope all sleep well.

Gators in the River

I N 2006, WHILE SERVING AS A CIVILIAN ADVISOR IN SOUTHERN Iraq, our little forward operating base (FOB) was located along a beautiful river. We had three-layer wire parameters and were guarded well, with the "weak" side being the river. There were folks swimming and bathing daily on the bank of the river in plain view. I always felt a little uneasy about that side of the compound; it seemed less secure than the rest of the FOB.

My son, Jim, had killed several gators back home and had sent photos that were taped to the side of my desk. With locals and soldiers coming by daily, there were many comments made in amazement. The locals seemed unusually excited about the photos and asked many questions.

Even though I was now working with the US State Department as a senior foreign field advisor, as I had retired from counterintelligence, I started formulating a lone-wolf plan. When coming back off leave from the States, before going back to work, I went down to the mess hall and got five dozen eggs, without any witnesses. I chose a room adjacent to my office and arranged the eggs in nests, staged incubation with light bulbs, and placed many photos of alligators around the room. I kept the door ajar and well lit day and night. Everyone who walked by could see that something was going on in that little room, but what was actually happening was a mystery all were curious about.

After several weeks, late one night I took the eggs outside and broke them, retaining only the shells. I stealthily spread the eggshells around the room, in the nests and on the floor. Those same "interested" people took notice, and word spread that the eggs had hatched, and the baby gators had taken refuge in the river beside the compound.

Throughout this time, I kept quiet. My "terps" (interpreters) relayed that there was talk in the town and throughout the entire area about the gators in the river. People were seen observing the waters, waiting to witness a gator. No longer were there bathers and swimmers along the opposite bank.

I never lied; I never said the eggs were gator eggs nor ever mentioned anything about gators at all. The folks coming and going by that room, seeing the photos and eggshells, drew their own conclusions.

When I came and went from my office building compound, I was pleased with my work and the success of my having nothing to do with the gators in the rivers of Iraq. I was just a country boy from North Florida, doing my best to entertain myself and polish my skills.

As far as I know, there are no American gators in Iraq, but there is one hell of a tale about them going around.

I Didn't Know What an Army Ranger Was

O N SLEEPLESS NIGHTS I THINK OUT LOUD. RANDOM thoughts. This is another one of those nights. Can't sleep, but I can maybe write a little story.

When I was twenty-three years old, I didn't give much thought to my weight if all else seemed to be okay. It certainly was not my intention to join an organization to lose weight, but join up I did, a complete volunteer.

I caught a bus in Tallahassee, and it wound its way up through the red plowed fields of the fine state of Georgia. Upon arriving at the designated location, I was met with a very warm welcome. The place had a camp-like appearance—well, more like a prison with many buildings built very much alike, something like out of a World War II movie. The friendly atmosphere didn't last long. These folks meant business. By the end of the first week, only about a third of us were still in the program. I seemed to be doing really well, in my mind, but they had a different opinion. We were sorrier than shit-eating dogs and lower than whale shit. I should have sensed that something was not right, but I had joined and was determined to finish what I had started. So off to some serious activities the following week.

More of my classmates kept going home. In the first two weeks, the people in my building had dwindled to half the number with which we started. We hardly ever saw that building after the first day; it was just a place to get maybe two or three hours of sleep in a twenty-four-hour day. As a side note, it was unbelievable what we had to do to get a meal that had to be eaten in a matter of minutes. In my building alone, we started with forty folks from all walks of life and from all over the country. The one commonality we had was that we were all determined to finish.

I was surprised that everyone was in such good shape, or so I thought. Our instructors were supermen—strong, dedicated to their mission, which I found out later was to put as many of us out as possible, or at least that was what it seemed. Their real mission was to allow only the best, mentally and physically most capable, and truly dedicated individuals to graduate.

I was catching on. I was confident in myself but worried I might turn an ankle or possibly come down with some sickness that would not allow me to finish. Hell, I had not crapped in three weeks, and that did worry me. How was that even possible? I never had any thoughts of giving up; however, I was seeing troubles in some of the others by the third week. Some fell out from the inability to complete tasks; others from not dedicating enough for this kind of life.

I could see it in their eyes and body language; they had given up. Within days, they would disappear. More than ever, I was determined to finish out this training. Early on I had gained recognition for being top for physical fitness. I had finished the brutal physical training test that first week in the fifth percentile of the same three hundred or so who had started. The first week they put us five-percenters in charge of the others—something that made it even harder on us mentally, which was their plan all along. Even during this grueling process, I continued to love it, but I still worried that something could always happen to me to put me out.

On the fourth week, we found ourselves only getting one meal per day, training some twenty-plus hours every day with no time-outs, holidays, or Sundays. To make matters worse, we were training in North Georgia in the foothill and mountain ridges. We were starting to have to skills related to our training. We were being graded on our leadership, ability to control situations and people, and ability to make things happen. Still, no breaks.

Into the fifth week, I met my first big hit. I nearly died of humiliation. I had received a failing grade on a task of which I was in charge. My people had not been able to handle the assignment, and as the leader I had failed them. I found myself in a long line of folks who had to wait to see the guy in charge. I'll never forget his name or appearance; he was a top professional and mean looking, like a rattlesnake crossed with a bulldog. He chewed tobacco, and kept one eye a little squinted as he talked, chewed, and spat at the same time.

When I reported inside that door of his makeshift office, Captain Rinsul looked at me like I was the white stuff on chickenshit. I was trying my best to look confident, had my chest pushed forward, standing ramrod straight, looking into his eyes, thinking he was going to jump at me any second. I will never ever forget his words. "Barbee, you from Tallahassee? If you fail another patrol, I will personally chase your ass back there, beating your ass all the way. Do you understand?" I answered in the affirmative and then the words came out of my mouth.

"Sir, you will not be chasing me back to Tallahassee or anywhere else," I said, with tears in my eyes, scared to death I might fail another. There are always so many things to take care of in a mission: logistics, personnel and their individual problems, the difficulty of planning for and carrying out a successful mission and keeping everyone safe, getting them back, all under extreme conditions of fatigue, distance, unknowns, limitations, shortages, dealing with all the communications, making hundreds of decisions, and making it all work to be ready for the next assignment. It all was never ending.

There was a scary silence in the room for a moment as the good captain considered what I said. I was wondering if I had run my mouth too much. Captain Rinsul then said, "Barbee, before you leave here you're going to be so bad you will be able to eat the rear end out of a menstruating shuck. Do you understand? I better not see you again in this office. Now get your ass out of here."

I saluted and replied, "Yes, sir." I even lost more than two hours of sleep that night thinking about what he said and worried that I might twist an ankle in the mountains.

Little did I know, everyone had failed their patrol in that time period. The mental pressure was in full force. If a prospect failed two patrols, he was toast, gone. I never looked back after that day. I had already lost over 25 pounds in five weeks. Their program was working, but when I started I was only 167 pounds at six feet tall. Oh well, I didn't know I had lost that much weight. I was still moving.

I was butt-deep in the US Army Ranger program, a weight-loss, mental-sharpening, and soldier-making program. I was learning, still feeling good physically, semi confident, but determined with very few doubts. I just had to make the right decisions and keep moving.

In the mountain phase, we learned even more about ourselves and others, and the soldier skills kept improving. The hectic pace never let up; we were averaging twenty-two and a half training hours a day with very little sleep. The sixteen left in my platoon were about to move into the Florida phase. Little did I know how much I didn't know. I felt blessed just being there; others had done this, so I could as well. I thought if I was kicked out of ranger school, I would never, ever be able to look anyone else in the eye again.

That patrol failure was the low point in my mental well-being, as it was designed to be. I overcame it and learned from it, but I would never spit in Captain Rinsul's eye. He had made me cry; I just hope he didn't notice. I know my eyes had to be red that day, but if a tear had rolled out and down my cheek I would have crapped. I can still see myself with those red eyes, standing at attention in front of the commander. There had been a long line behind me and in front of me that day, but that was no consolation as they were failures too. There is a reason for failures—learn and grow in order to never fail again.

I made it through the Florida phase and graduated to become a US Army Ranger, and that has served me well throughout my life so far.

We started with some great soldiers; they were all first-rate soldiers out of the regular army, and some were not ready for that type of training for some reason—maybe skill levels, mental or physical ability, attitude, or whatever. Some were medically removed, some were just unlucky, some failed peer ratings, others disappeared and I never knew why. The good Lord just had something else for them, and most went on to very successful careers.

There were many interesting stories to be told about what all happens to someone in ranger school, and one day I hope to tell about some of them; this little story was a different view. I didn't know what an Army Ranger was, and I became one.

Note: At graduation I weighed 127 pounds. Exactly 329 soldiers started the class, and only 87 finished—40 in my platoon started; 9 graduated. God had a plan for me. Ready or not, here I come.

Another tale from a sleepless night.

Just Another Day in Iraq

O N THE DAY IN IRAQ THAT MAJOR ED EVERSMAN'S CONVOY
was attacked, I was stuck in heavy traffic, returning from
the Iraqi Ministry of Agriculture.

In my convoy were three armored Humvees and my vehicle, a
Nissan SUV nontactical vehicle (NTV) with tinted windows. As I
always did on such a movement in built-up areas, I led from the front.

Here leading from the front was not because of the old Ranger
adage, "Lead from the front," but because a vehicle such as the SUV
in the middle of a military convey usually is the higher-profile target.
With a civilian vehicle in the lead, the public and others usually
looked past the civilian vehicle to the military vehicles. The SUV
doesn't look like it's part of the convoy. I never saw anyone looking
at my vehicle while in this configuration.

The turret gunner in the second vehicle provided critical
overwatch.

On this particular day, we had attended and were returning from
a cabinet-level meeting at the ministry. I was driving this vehicle
with our coalition civil affairs counterpart from the Ukraine, Colonel
Alex, designated as codriver, and the Ukrainian ambassador was in
the back seat.

We had been stuck in slow four-to-five-lane traffic for well over
twenty minutes. We were moving much too slowly, which is a security
problem. There was no way to nose in and out of the tight traffic on
that day, not even if a Humvee had been in the lead. We were on the
inside lane next to a one-foot-high and about ten-inch-wide median

barrier. Needless to say, with so many Iraqi pedestrians and vehicles all around us, we were all a little nervous in this slow traffic.

As the driver, I had a clear view down the right-side lane of the oncoming vehicles as well as down the median. About forty to fifty meters ahead, in the oncoming lane, was a brown-and-gold-colored civilian vehicle, with a very excited person in civilian attire waving an unrecognizable weapon out the driver's side passenger window.

If that vehicle continued toward us, that person and weapon would be within one to two yards of my window. I found out later the weapon was a Sterling submachine gun.

I alerted Alex and the ambassador and told them the situation: in just a few minutes, there was going to be a vehicle, with a person waving a weapon, to my left front and for them to open their doors and prepare to exit on their right, move back to the rear vehicles, and stay low.

As the driver, I was sort of trapped. If they were bad guys, which we all thought they had to be, something was about to happen. Looking into my rear view mirror, the turret gunner was not looking ahead. His attention was properly directed at the tops of buildings and the storefronts and alleys. I handed Alex an AK-47, which I kept at my right side by the console. As I shifted my Beretta to my left hand, I asked the ambassador if he wanted a pistol. The ambassador replied he did. Alex, now armed with the AK-47, handed him his pistol.

What was about to happen was going to be very close. While all this was going on, the traffic in my lane was at a standstill. The opposite lane traffic was barely moving, but the vehicle was getting closer. I knew if the turret gunner saw what I saw he would be in motion in seconds. Just at that moment, the brown-and-gold-colored vehicle turned to their right and cut down a side alley. As they were turning, I saw the brown suburban and a very excited American-looking guy waving what looked like an automatic weapon. They then sped down a side alley at a high rate of speed. It was one of our special operations teams; they had just been ambushed ten minutes earlier.

I saw no other activity, and I told Alex that they had looked like Americans, that something must have happened up the road in front of us, and to stay prepared. The occupants in that vehicle had been excited about something, maybe an ambush, or their concern may have been about people in another vehicle.

Our convey moved on slowly through the traffic, and we watched for problems, as we always did, but this time we were much more alert.

It wasn't until later in the day, upon returning to our billeting compound, that I heard about Major Eversman's running ambush and realized that was who we had seen. Major Eversman was coming back into Baghdad after his two vehicles had been in a running attack ten minutes earlier, and their adrenaline was still high. Three of the attackers, I understand, were shot and fell out of their vehicle while traveling around eighty miles per hour.

I've thought about that day many times, wondering if my vehicle being in the lead was tactically the right thing to do.

Yes, on that day, on that movement, it was the right call.

My Hog Went to
Iraq and Back

U PON RECEIVING NOTIFICATION THAT MY UNIT WAS GOING
to Iraq, my ADD mind immediately went into overdrive.
What was I going to need, beyond the essentials? What could I
take that would be most useful and provide the most value? What
would I consider necessary to spice up the flavor of life in a war
zone?

Iraq was a unique country, one with a different faith, culture, and
people. It is a Muslim nation with deep roots in Islam. What would
I need to bring with me?

As I thought about it, the answer became clear: I'll need a
mounted hog's head, my bow and arrows, a few cans of lard, and
maybe some southern ways to take with me.

I was the chief of intelligence, the G-2, for the task force, a job
that was viewed by many as an important staff position, one usually
held in high regard because the officer in that role was generally very
bright. Well, I figured I might be an exception to that rule, but if I
kept my mouth shut and listened a lot, maybe nodded in agreement
every once in a while—sort of like a no-account doctor, a friend of
mine, Doc Canale—I might just get by.

One big advantage I had was that I generally loved my job as
a soldier, but more specifically I loved being an intel officer. I had
also been a counterintelligence officer, so I liked watching people,
figuring out what they might be thinking and how they might react
to different situations. It turns out those things fit well with another

of my favorite pastimes—figuring out how to find the lighter side of life and how to make the best of a bad situation.

In that regard, it helps to have people around who feel the same way. A good example is my cousin, Lieutenant Colonel Rob Parrish, who was also in my unit and just happens to be a world-renowned head doctor—he says "neurosurgeon"—out in Houston. Rob's a serious professional who literally makes life-or-death decisions every day.

As we prepared to deploy to Iraq, this brilliant surgeon and Blountstown native stuck his head in my door and asked an important question: "Logan, what was the name I used back when I was a professional wrestler?"

Before I get on with the hog story, I should probably explain how that conversation came about.

As the G-2 for the unit, my duty was making sure everyone had appropriate security clearances—helping folks get them or taking them away, if necessary. That morning, several new colonels who had been assigned to the unit for this deployment had to have their clearances upgraded. So, early that morning we four colonels drove out to the local navy base to get them "read on" and sworn in.

These guys didn't know me from Adam's house cat. All they knew was that I was the colonel in charge of the intelligence section of the unit and the deployment. I saw my chance to impress them with my southern wit and intellect.

As it happened, they were talking about various folks in the unit, and they had already met LTC Parrish, so I thought I would help them get to know Rob a little better.

I said, "Oh, y'all have met my cousin LTC Parrish." I showed my excitement and pride in him being my cousin. I also decided to spice up Rob's backstory a little—remember: it can't be all serious. At the same time, I wanted them to get a good first impression of their new chief of intelligence, on whom their futures might depend.

So I started piling it on thick: Rob and I went to high school together, and he was a much better student than most of his peers, including me. Rob was also a popular guy in high school, great athlete, but he quit football to pursue a professional wrestling career. The entire school and our entire family were extremely proud of him, even if it nearly destroyed the attendance at the local football games. See, every Friday night, instead of going to our local football games, half of the town convoyed up to Dothan, Alabama, to the watch "the Rock" wrestle.

Rob always went into the ring with a mask on because he figured if wrestling didn't work out he might want to do something else. Little did we know, he had medical ambitions. Of course, we were terribly disappointed that he chose to go into medicine, but I guess it's worked out okay for him—and us too. Half of the family has been to Houston for some free head work, and we all got to see Texas.

Needless to say, I noticed some eyes rolling during the trip, but I never let up. I meant to let them know I was just kidding, but I forgot all about telling them. All this to say, I forgot about it right up until a couple of days later, when Rob checked in the 2-shop to ask what his wrestling name was.

As far as I know, Rob never gave me up, and I can only imagine what they were saying about the crazy intel officer and his wrestler-doctor cousin. It doesn't matter, though, because they all got the proper introduction I had planned.

Colonel K, a lawyer, had heard a rumor, so he sidled into my office and asked in a sly, quiet voice, with his head tilted slightly, "Logan, you are not taking a hog head to Iraq, are you?"

"Where in the world did you hear that?" I asked.

He got defensive and told me he had "just heard it." I told him I had thought about it, but that I was offered six cans of lard in trade, so it didn't look like the old boar was going to make the trip.

As he was leaving, I followed up, "If you hear any more rumors, don't hesitate to stop by and ask. It's my job to check into things like that." I said it with all the seriousness I could muster. Not surprisingly, that was the last I heard about the issue from Colonel K, and I don't even think he knew anything about lard.

Somehow it didn't seem strange to me to be taking a hog head and six cans of lard to Iraq. Everybody takes a little piece of home with them when they leave. My piece just had more tusks and wiry hair than others. It helped that I was prior enlisted, so I was less concerned with the letter of the law than the spirit. And as far as I was concerned, the spirit definitely wanted me to have my hog with me.

So I got the magnificent mounted boar's head packed up, loaded into one of our CONEX containers, and shipped out to Iraq ahead of us. It must have been a lonely trip for him, cramped up in that container, not knowing what was in store for him. It was surely different than home.

I acquired the old boar from Mr. George Burch, a local Calhoun County legend, who was a taxidermist by trade, among other specialties. George was a real southern character and truth-teller, and I'll write some more about him later, when I explain how I got my hog back from Iraq. In fact, there are a lot of stories I need to share about George.

I hope he was as proud of his work as I was. That old boar's head found his way into many adventures in Iraq, and he did it with flare and a half grin the entire time. I regret not giving him a name, because he never missed a step during his time in-country. The best

I can do instead is share some of his stories. Not all of them—that might not be good for either one of us.

On one occasion, the boar showed up at the First Iraq International Invitational Archery Championship. He kept watch over our compound, scared buggers away, and was a companion on several outings in and around Baghdad. Not one time was he ever shown anything but great respect from the folks who shared his presence.

Sometimes he appeared on the front door of the palace. Many locals didn't seem to know what to do, and I suspect it confirmed our reputation as American infidels. Believe it or not, however, even the Iraqis showed him respect, no matter what their beliefs.

I may be wrong, but I dare say he may have been the only American wild boar to ever visit Iraq. One might say it was his first Iraqi rodeo, and now that I think about it he may have made history. I might just try and get him inducted into the National Hog Hall Wall of Fame (NHHWF). If that doesn't exist, I might create it.

In any event, getting the hog into Iraq had been easy. That's because moving material into a war zone is a usually a more-is-better proposition, but the powers that be get a little more careful about what comes back home.

I knew there would be increased scrutiny for the return trip, but by now I was pretty sure I could pull it off. Heck, I bluffed my way through as the chief of intelligence for an entire year in a foreign country at war. How hard could it be to get a hog's head back home from Iraq?

As it happens, the answer is very hard. The army and every other federal agency, it seemed, had strict rules about transporting animals, even stuffed ones, out of country. But I wasn't about to leave my furry buddy pinned down under a pile of red tape.

When it looked like I wouldn't get approval to bring him back, I took off like the house was on fire. My first stop was the US embassy, where I retrieved—sometimes I say "repositioned"—several ink pads and rubber stamps off one the secretary's desks, along with a few sheets of stationery. The paper had "US Embassy" stamped on it to help me appear official. To make it even more valid, I asked one the translators for some old Iraqi papers that were typed in Arabic.

My next stop was to find one of the unit's officers, who was a veterinarian in civilian life. He gave me a letter of clearance for transporting the head back to the States. I had the mounted hog's head fumigated, wrapped tightly in several garbage bags, then put into an opened box. Now came the moment of truth.

The inspector who was clearing us out of Iraq was heading my way. I was next to have my gear and belongings inspected. As he and I came to the box with the mount, tightly bound and sealed, he asked, "What's in the bag?" I told him it was a hog's head as I retrieved the packet of papers from the box and handed them to him.

He gave me a look that said, "Well, this is a first," as he thumbed through the inch-thick packet of papers with letters from the US embassy, an American veterinarian, and the Iraqi ministries of agriculture, health, and interior. He even had one letter from George Burch, taxidermist from Calhoun County, that vouched that the head had originated in the United States and was certified, correctly mounted, and federally approved.

To be honest, I have no idea what the Arabic letters said. I do know that nothing was incriminating in the other letters, but I can guarantee they had nothing to do with shipping a hog's head out of Iraq.

The only legitimate letter was from the veterinarian, stating it was fumigated and ready for shipment. The inked stamps from the embassy made it all look plenty authentic and impressive.

I was a little disappointed that the inspector never even wanted to look at my prized boar. He just shook his head, handed the papers back, and said, "Pack it all up and load it into that container." I complied, of course, but I still felt like he deserved a better send-off, especially given all he contributed during his service.

My fellow officers and soldiers who got to know the old boar really seemed to like him. They were amazed he was able to get to Iraq on his own, just to boost our morale and share our hardships. I think those kindred souls who witnessed his arrival and felt his presence at certain functions were better for the experience.

For his part, the old hog enjoyed a position of prestige during his twelve-plus months in Iraq. Those of us he served with can attest to his loyalty, his selfless reasons for being there, and his real dedication to his American upbringing. He has now been put to pasture in my office on a sacred and honored wall, where he is surrounded by framed photos of American heroes, of whom he is considered—by some—to be one.

Oh, about that letter from George Burch: I emailed the Calhoun County Extension Office and explained my dilemma. I said I needed a letter from George noting that the mounted boar's head originated in the United States, that it had been mounted professionally by an accredited, licensed taxidermist, that I had bought and paid for the mount, and had indeed transported the same with me to Iraq.

It seemed simple enough, but I think George might have smelled a rat. He didn't get to be a legendary character for nothing. The bottom line is that George crawfished on me, and I have my suspicions as to why. The story did seem a little wild, or maybe George hadn't renewed his license. Or it might be he just didn't want to get involved with some foreign shenanigans.

Whatever the reason, I still loved George—he, after all, held legend status—and his country suspicions. But I couldn't let that keep my brother-hog-at-arms from getting home. So I made up some letterhead with the University of Florida logo, Calhoun County Extension Office, and wrote a letter for George's signature.

I never told George when I returned, but he sure wrote a great letter, and it helped me save my boar's head. Looking back, I wished I had told him. George always enjoyed a good story, and I think he would be proud to know what an important role he played in the war effort, even if part of it was without his knowledge.

Maybe he and General Black Jack Pershing are looking down now and smiling about the effect a well-employed pig can have in wartime.

As I said, I regret not giving my old boar a proper name, but maybe some readers can help. Any suggestions?

Rambling Thoughts
of Gratitude

I N MY PAST, I'VE BEEN FORTUNATE TO HAVE EXPERIENCED A
few things in life that have given me many reasons to be
appreciative of life and to be appreciative of the assistance of others.
For the several years that I was operating in Iraq, I was assisted
and protected by a group of professionals who some people felt
were over the top, overpaid, and overaggressive. I found many who
didn't appreciate them and were very critical of their performance—
mostly "snowflakes." But I, for one, admired their performance,
professionalism, dedication to our country, and their high level of
engagement.

From someone looking at their performance from a distance,
I can understand because I also had the same feeling at times. I
saw them as too aggressive, wild, overpaid, difficult to understand,
and sometimes it seemed like they caused more problems than they
solved.

Blackwater contractors and others like them are in reference
here. The last year or so, while serving in Iraq with the US State
Department as a senior advisor to our military, the new Iraqi
government, and Iraqi citizens, I was fortunate to be able to get
a firsthand view of these Blackwater and other contractor "boys"
in action. At all times, day and night, they provided security and
protection for the advisors and foreign service personnel at the FOBs
we were assigned to.

Each day we ventured out to meet with Iraqi government

officials, tribal leaders, business people, Iraqi citizen groups, or our military in the field. We usually traveled in four to five armored civilian Suburbans in convoy, routed through the countryside to get to our destination. There were always twelve to sixteen Blackwater personnel in the detail, always traveling at high rates of speed, with very deliberate actions and movements, always alert to their surroundings, highly sensitive to the operations of the day, and quick to react to different situations. On the journey to our destination, upon arrival, and on our return to safe harbor, Blackwater contractors proved to be very effective at their chosen profession.

From my viewpoint, I had the finest group of patriotic American combat-experienced professionals imaginable. They put themselves out front and accepted the terms of their duties with as much vigor and professionalism as I have ever seen. They were a sight to watch, and it was unbelievable to think about their dangerous and seemingly reckless maneuvering they had to do for some foreign, sometimes unfriendly actor.

Blackwater contractors and other contractor companies I had the privilege to get to know and to serve with were from small towns and cities across the United States and were former combat soldiers or marines with a variety of special training and skills. All had families and friends back in the States wondering just what in the heck they did for a living.

I had gratitude and an overwhelming feeling toward our military personnel when I worked and traveled with them, and these feelings continue to this day. They are all America's children, doing work far beyond anything they or I ever imagined doing. What an honor it was to have served with them and to have watched them in their endeavors in such dire, strenuous conditions and in dangerous places. I wish everyone could go for a ride with our "kids" through the backstreets and highways while representing the United States, trying to assist and help people all over the world. What courage, what fortitude, what confidence, what a belief in what they were doing. I wish I could express the feeling of sharing their comradeship, their professional bearing, and their most noble endeavors while moving through the night with others who haven't seen it or felt it. America is truly blessed, and I'm thankful for our soldiers. They are our children—America's children.

Good night. May we all sleep safely because of what they do.

SSPP: Supersecret
Pigeon Project

O UR UNIT MEMBERS AND STAFF WERE SEATED IN A LARGE auditorium at Fort Bragg, North Carolina, being briefed on activities and programs we could expect when arriving in Iraq. One of our new commander's ideas was to build within the unit and launch a new high-tech application. The program was for reporting back to him while deployed in the field. Needless to say, the folks around me and I looked at each other and rolled our eyes. We had enough reporting to do without generating more paperwork.

With no one standing up and denouncing the project, we would usually let it run its course. But I went and opened my big mouth to trusted friends. "I'll have homing pigeons flying before that will ever work or be deployed." It was a tongue-in-cheek idea.

That's how many of my side adventures start, with my mouth running without thinking. Now I have to finish deploying into a theater and somehow do my thing with homing pigeons, of which I knew nothing about at the time.

Note to readers: It's all about me following up on my overloaded ADD and mouth running; I now think I have to save face and make it all happen, or else I'm just another loudmouth who doesn't perform. Well, I like to think of myself as a top performer, even if it is in the bull hockey arena. So here is the story of the SSPP (supersecret pigeon project), which morphed into the JSSPP (joint SSPP), then to the CJSSPP (combined joint SSPP), of which I am proud of, knowing that my BH was in top form. It is important to know I never told a lie about the project. As always, I left that up to others to spread word of the project throughout the underworld grapevine. All I did was create many assumptions and left unanswered questions so many were confused about whether it was right or not. This is all dangerous work in the military—to pull off satire within the command. One could have been court-martialed for some of the pranks I've pulled. But sometimes the side work is worth the effort and risk just to get folks thinking. Also, the project was a good morale booster, as the soldiers loved the idea. I was just thinking like my old enlisted self. Loved it.

Well, as soon as we got into the theater—Iraq—and were settled into our prospective jobs, it was time to go to work, so I mixed business with pleasure by talking with the locals and researching homing pigeons. Come to find out, we had a homing-pigeon expert in the unit, a sergeant who knew his stuff. He, along with the computer, taught me a significant amount.

First of all, I acquired a few cages from Saddam's zoo that he maintained close to the National Palace, which was beside the Republican Guards' housing. By the way, that is where the $365 million was found, hidden behind cemented walls. There were $4 million per box, but we'll save the money story for another time.

Next I found a local who had the feed, pigeons, and chicken wire for sale. I made my first local purchase in Iraq. I set the cages up down by the motor pool so the soldiers could witness the progress, and they were a great help in maintaining the pigeons. They took a great interest in the pigeons' welfare and kept the project low-key.

Soon the project started to build and grow, in more ways than one. There were eggs everywhere, and the pigeons started sitting. Before long, little pigeons were everywhere.

To say I was a little afraid of losing the birds is an understatement.

I wouldn't let the birds go out at first, afraid they would not come back. So I created a small illusion. I typed out messages to create the idea that the pigeons had been working and flying already. I left the notes and capsules made from sections cut from ink pens, with the notes rolled up, sticking out of them on top of cages.

Everyone was a witness to the progress of the Supersecret Pigeon Project (SPP). Some messages read: "All clear at GF109938838 crossroads; have setup send beer at VC 27666888987." I still feel bad about not telling anyone about the phony notes and capsules I left on the cages, but everyone got to see them, and word spread in underground networks that the SPP was working and very successful.

I even did a PowerPoint briefing on it for fun, detailing the CAkMS versus SPP. The SSPP was low cost, self-replicating, had been a working system for hundreds of years, was unsuspected by the enemy, and was a morale booster. And I wasn't caught and court-martialed. All in all, it was becoming a roaring success. Then the marines heard about the joint SPP, then the Brits wanted in, so it morphed into the Combined Joint Supersecret Pigeon Project (CJSPP). I was going to jail, and I knew it, but no, everyone kept it under wraps. It was our little secret and humor at the expense of the big brass.

I never did have to tell any lies about the project; it grew on its own weight. Folks wanted to believe the little man could prevail against city hall, and we can.

The First Annual Bosnia International Invitational Longbow Championship

When my boys were growing up, while learning how to shoot their first bows and rifles, they were taught shooting instinctively with iron sights first. After they became proficient while shooting without sight pins and optics, they could train using other sights. When they asked if they could get a scope, I would reply, "That's sorta like cheating." I would make a cross with my two pointer figures and say, "If all you have to do is place the crosshairs on a target and pull the trigger, who can't do that? Even the target is magnified."

I had a group of youngsters, up to twenty at times, who I would take to 3D archery tournaments. Their ages ranged from six to sixteen. Our ragtag bunch would usually bring home a majority of the trophies. I would listen to their conversations during and after the tournaments. At one tournament, my middle child came up to me and said, "Every time we shoot, there is usually a group watching, and they say, 'Looks like these kids don't even shoot with sights.'" The youngsters were proud of their skills and abilities against pin-sight shooters.

But like all kids growing up, they recognized that their shooting accuracy would improve with pin sights. Peer pressure was weighing on them and me, as we all wanted them to advance their skills. They won even more trophies with the advanced sights.

So after years of coaching kids in archery and organizing and participating in tournaments, I learned a great deal.

So here the story begins: My unit was called up to be deployed into Bosnia and Herzegovina, a war zone, for a twelve-to-thirteen-month deployment.

Upon arrival in Bosnia, my unit, the 350 Civil Affairs Command, numbering three-hundred-plus soldiers, was deployed throughout the theater. We settled into our jobs and began learning the ways and culture of a new country and how to operate. As usual, days ran hot and cold—sometimes busy with soldiering and other times boring, leading to thoughts of home.

I was on staff as the chief intelligence officer for the command, and my staff and I stayed very busy. This was the first time—that anyone knew of—that a Special Operations Civil Affairs unit was using its intelligence staff to collect information, albeit passive. It was against our unit's doctrine to collect intelligence, but recognizing that we fit a unique position in the country. The three-lettered agencies had very few assets or resources in the country, and we had officers, NCOs, and soldiers throughout the country located in very high government positions. So passive information and intelligence gathering was within our scope. Therefore, my team and I went to work on a unique mission, setting precedents for other units in the future and fulfilling a very important role of providing intelligence information from the theater of operations.

Even though we were extremely busy, I found out many years earlier that if I wanted something done I had give it to the busy, energetic people, and that task would be done as well. But no one gave us this plan or any of the other projects and activities we, as a section, engaged in. We just did our thing and set about making Bosnia a little more like home and to cheer things up a bit.

We planted gardens, planned and organized youth soccer matches, organized and attended the national theater and other cultural events. We planned Christmas and New Year's Eve events, attended underground theater performances that the troops could actually participate in. One might say my staff became the informal morale and support committee for the troops housed in and around Sarajevo.

One grand event we came up with was the First Annual Bosnia International Invitational Longbow Championship. Before much planning could be done, we had to acquire the equipment and tools to put on such an event.

One day I was thumbing through an old archery publication brought over from the States. A small advertisement caught my eye. It was a paid ad by the Jerry Hill Archery Company. I'll never forget the call I made to a town in Wilsonville, Alabama. Someone at the other end of the call picked up and said, "Hello."

My first comment was, "I'm calling from Sarajevo, Herzegovina."

The guy at the other end of the line replied, "You calling from where?"

I said again, "Sarajevo," and then said, "I understand y'all make outstanding long bows."

He said, "We make the best."

My next comments might have sounded a little unusual. "We're putting on an international longbow tournament here, and we need a bow and arrows. And if we get one of yours, I will guarantee you that your bow will be the top-rated bow, and with it first place will be taken."

I still didn't know who I was talking to, but the guy at the other end of the line asked, "How can you guarantee that?"

To that I replied, "Yours will be the only bow in the tournament."

There was silence on the line, then a little chuckle, and he said, "What do you need?"

I told him to send me a good bow and a dozen or so arrows, with tips and extra flexing, nocks, etc.

About three weeks later, a rather large box arrived for my section, and it was filled with videotapes, magazines, archery supplies, and a beautiful Jerry Hill signature laminated wood longbow with arrows to go with it. We began setting dates and planning. Also, practice for many non-shooters began.

Many of our soldiers, as well as several locals, Turkish soldiers, and contractor civilians, practiced with that bow before the event. We ordered trophies and developed a poster advertisement for the event.

I and a few others had the habit of practicing at daylight before chow in the mornings. In doing so, several of the Turkish gate guards began watching the practice with curiosity. One morning I thought I would see if a broadhead would penetrate protective gear, which it did. After shooting into the vest at about fifteen yards, I looked up and saw the guard curiously watching—he with an automatic weapon across his chest, and me with a wood longbow and arrows. I looked at him and patted the bow with my hand as I held it up on my chest. The guard, in turn, patted his weapon and smiled back. I just patted the bow again and then placed my pointing figure over my mouth and said, "Shush," the international motion for indicating quiet sounding, as I was using silent and deadly arrows. The guard just patted his weapon and walked away, still guarding the gate.

The event day was very successful. We held the main tournament and a William Tell event consisting of shooting an apple sitting on top of a cardboard cutout head for cash prizes. Over thirty participated in the tournament, all shooting a right-handed Jerry Hill signature longbow. The first-, second-, and third-place winners received trophies, and all received certificates that they participated in a world-class archery event.

I don't remember the placing, except one: I came in fifth place. After all, I was a left-handed shooter using a right-handed bow. All in all, everyone seemed to have had an enjoyable day.

I appreciate Jerry Hill for helping a bunch of homesick GIs in a war zone enjoy a day of archery many miles from home.

Notes: One soldier in my section received her degree when she returned to the States; her internship for graduation from a university was interrupted by this deployment. Because I was an associate professor with the University of Florida, I contacted the soldier's professor, and she was able to intern in Bosnia and complete in-service training in an international war zone. I believe her degree was recreation and leisure sports. I understand the soldier gave presentations on her internship to many groups at the request of her professor.

Also, in 2005, the unit was deployed to Iraq, where I participated in and helped to facilitate the First Iraqi International Invitational Archery Championship.

Weapons to the Ministry

Most of the Iraqi ministry personnel had been trained and were to be issued handguns and ammunition for their self-protection by the US military. But the Ministry of Agriculture, to which I was the senior US advisor, still had no security or any way to defend itself in the event of an attack. This was important because ministries were often attacked with small arms and with explosive devices placed in or around compounds.

Being concerned for the safety of the minister and staff personnel and the visitors to the agriculture ministry, I made an inquiry into how to acquire the weapons and ammo more quickly. One of our civil affairs personnel was assigned to facilitate the deliveries, so I contacted Major Eversman. He was most helpful and immediately cleared the way for me to assist in getting the arms to the ministry, and with his help I began making the preparations.

Moving arms is always serious business, especially in a war zone. To conduct the operation securely, I scheduled a five-vehicle convoy of armored Humvees, with a team of armed soldiers to escort us to the pickup point, secure the weapons and ammo, and then deliver them to the correct personnel at the ministry. I requested from our headquarters a heavy-duty vehicle, such as a five-ton military truck, with a driver, an armed assistant driver, and a shooter.

On the day of the scheduled convoy, the armored vehicle I had requested showed up on time in the green zone parking lot, and the convoy commander reported to me. I told him I was waiting for the heavy vehicle and three soldiers to haul the supplies we were going to deliver. About ten minutes before departure time, here came a commercial flatbed truck with side panels and one of our unit soldiers driving. Nineteen-year-old Private Cody Geiger had volunteered to go, and the first sergeant had no other personnel available.

Instead of my military five-ton, here I stood with only a commercial-grade paneled truck and a young driver, about to travel to the Iraqi Police Academy armory—one of the most likely ambush destinations in Baghdad. But the mission was critical because the ministry officials would grow more vulnerable if word spread they were unarmed and undefended. A handful of soldiers from my unit were standing around, so I asked for volunteers to take on this dicey assignment.

Lieutenant Colonel David Cunningham and a sergeant volunteered. Cunningham got into the back of the flatbed, and the sergeant got into the assistant driver's seat. I was climbing into the back of the flatbed with Cunningham as the convoy commander came up and said, "Colonel Barbee, I have a seat for you in one of the armored Humvees."

My reply was that I would prefer riding in the flatbed, if he didn't mind making the changes. He, being a good NCO, said, "Yes, sir," and returned to the convoy and handled its movement to the designated locations.

I should explain that often a sergeant is designated as the convoy commander, not the highest-ranking officer. But I'm sure he had never seen two colonels riding in the back of a truck in a war zone. My guess is that he was wondering how he was going to explain that if something happened.

Cunningham and I settled down in the back of the flatbed as we began our journey. Many things crossed my mind that day and the days since. Two colonels were riding shotgun security in the bed of a commercial vehicle going many, many miles to several dangerous locations, loaded with arms and ammo.

That day I was in a long-sleeve blue shirt with a tie, khakis, and brown boots, which was not the typical attire for a soldier in a combat theater, especially one riding in the back of a flatbed truck in the middle of a steel dragon convoy. But here we went.

Some might ask about my judgment or my sanity, but this was a time when coming up through the ranks as I had turned out to be invaluable. I knew this was going to be a learning experience for all of us, but most especially the nineteen-year-old driving that commercial truck. He was willing to put himself on the line, and I knew from my own experience that I would be setting an example for him.

The convoy maneuvered several miles out to the academy, where we were greeted by scenes of damage and destruction to the entrance and gate areas from past bombings and attacks. Once inside, we found the armory and secured two hundred weapons and well over one hundred thousand rounds of ammo. While we were there, I noticed several cases of bayonets stacked inside. When I asked about them, the Iraqi contractor looked up and asked, "Would you like a footlocker of them?"

He and his men carried and slid a full footlocker of AK-47 bayonets and scabbards into the back of the flatbed. It's important to note that these items were not listed on the manifest, so I thanked him, and our convoy headed on to the ministry.

When we arrived, I left Private Geiger in charge of distributing the weapons and ammo, instructing him to get a signature so we could account for each one. I then left Geiger and the other soldiers as guards for the transaction and went inside to meet with the minister and give a report of the day's activities. Obviously, they were very, very thankful for newfound security and the ability to defend themselves in case of an attack.

Around seven hours after the journey began, we returned to the beginning point, with no incidents to report on that day, except that we had accomplished our mission.

I rode back over to the headquarters with Private Geiger, and we drove into the unit's motor pool area. Geiger, who usually didn't get to go out into the red zone, had had a very exciting day. He told me very enthusiastically that if I ever needed anyone to go out to please call on him. The young Geiger types are what make America great, and he's made of real American grit. The least I could have done for him and all those like him was ride in the back that day. Private Cody Geiger was a good soldier.

So I did a little more.

I removed a few of the bayonets out of the chest and shoved the rest of a load of souvenirs from Saddam's armory back into the bed of the truck. I said, "Geiger, these are yours," and suggested that he share some of them with the other soldiers and maybe take some home, if he didn't mind.

He thanked me and said, "Yes, sir."

I walked out of the motor pool, heading to the chow hall, thinking what a good day it had been.

Our enlisted soldiers are still the best. It makes me so proud every time I think of what they do.

May God bless our military.

Note: Today Cody Geiger is the 350th CACOM logistics management specialist during the week as a civilian and the HHC 350th 1SG as a reservist. He has over seventeen years in the service now. He has a beautiful wife, Ames Pepper, and one handsome five-year-old boy named Carson.

GOD WAS IN IRAQ

I N 2003 ABOUT 26 MILLION PEOPLE LIVED IN IRAQ, SOME 6 million of them in Baghdad. Among the city's residents was a majority of the nation's 1.2 million Christians. Under Saddam, Baghdad was very much a secular city, and many of those Christians lived in and around the green zone. This is where the National Iraqi Palace was located. Saddam trusted the Christians. He surrounded himself with them mainly because they were predictable and trustworthy. They did his cooking, housecleaning, and coexisted with him. On the other hand, the rival Muslim tribes and their leaders were unpredictable and often hostile, or maybe they were predictable in that their loyalty could be bought.

On my first tour of duty in Iraq, I had the good fortune to have an interpreter named Knenos Closeby, who had a cross tattooed between his thumb and first finger. He was a Christian, a keeper of the faith, and a good son of Iraqi Christian culture.

Knenos and his family were Aramaic. Their ancient language was the language in which the Bible was first written. We were talking one day, and he was telling me about his family and church. There were five or six Christian churches within the city limits of Baghdad. Knenos explained that his bishop had been saving old biblical manuscripts, biblical writings of scholars, and old Bibles for many years to protect them. His bishop was concerned that this archaeological biblical treasure might be lost to the world.

I offered to assist his church and bishop, without jeopardizing them with my association, if they would allow me to do so. The next day Knenos brought in an ancient book written in what appeared to be Arabic, bound by hand with leather covers. I examined the book wearing rubber medical gloves, which Knenos thought strange until I explained they were to protect the rare book. Afterward I gave him several boxes of gloves to take back to the bishop so this precaution could be continued.

Knenos suggested I keep the book awhile, and I reluctantly agreed. I wanted to examine it further and have it checked for authenticity and historical significance. But I also didn't want to be responsible for jeopardizing its integrity or endangering my friend and his church.

After some investigating, I found an American lieutenant colonel who was a paleographer—a professional who studied ancient manuscripts—in his civilian life. Fortunately, he was in Iraq, and I was able to contact him through his unit and request his assistance. The officer showed up in a couple of days and authenticated the book as over five hundred years old, hand bound, and printed using an ancient machine—not handwritten as I first thought. He was very impressed with the heretofore unknown ancient manuscripts and writings. As far as anyone knew, this book had never been seen outside the Arab world.

That discovery set off a chain of events in my office. We acquired some money to make digital copies of the manuscripts in order to protect them from the elements. We also kept this story quiet to protect the Iraqi Christians and their church. That meant we also kept our distance and were careful to not be seen there.

Eventually, the bishop and his staff acquired a document-photo camera, plastic gloves for handling materials, closed glass cabinets to store the manuscripts in, and an air conditioner to control the humidity. I sent electronic copies of the materials to Utah, New York, Washington, and to the UK and Italy. In fact, I sent them to any Christian seminary that I could locate that might study these priceless artifacts.

We never reported our actions up the chain of command nor did we ever say anything to the press. I did make a PowerPoint of the process just to record what we did and how we did it.

Just two weeks after I rotated back to the States, I learned that my friend Knenos had been kidnapped, tortured, and held for ransom by the bad guys. His father paid big money—something on the order of $20,000—and he was returned. It turns out, though, they were really looking for the American advisor he had worked with in the red and green zones.

There is a God, and he watches after crazies, babies, and foolish folks. It was not my time. God has a plan, but we just don't know it.

Later I heard Knenos was a refugee in Jordan, and I actually got to see him again in the lobby of a hotel there several years later. I was on my way back to Iraq, and we had an hour or so to catch up before I had to continue my journey. Knenos looked good and said he was doing okay but was worried about family members. My hope is that God will watch out for him and his loved ones, just as I pray for God to bless our military, our nation, and the foolish folks out there.

Note: The week after my unit left Iraq, we heard the Christian churches were targeted by the bad guys and that several were heavily damaged by explosions. Interestingly, the American military never spent much time at the Christian churches so as not to show partiality.

LAST ROCKET AND
MORTAR ATTACK

I SAW, HEARD, AND FELT MY FIRST MORTARS IN VIETNAM IN 1969. I was in the merchant marines—this was prior to being drafted into the US Army. As I traveled the world for over forty more years, I experienced many more attacks along the way in five real-life declared war zones—some multiple times. I even faced hostilities in a few places where war was not declared.

This little tale is going to be about my last rocket and mortar attack, along with a few reflections and my take on life.

There I sat, late at night, around 2400 hours (midnight), sitting on top of a bunker outside a regional FOB deep inside Iraq, close to the Iranian border.

I was waiting for an all-clear notice so that I could get back into the safety of the security compound. It was a beautiful starry night, with showers of fireworks popping, flaring, and lighting the late-night sky in the distance as our return fire hit the bad guys' suspected locations. Those same bad guys had just showered us with heavy mortar and rocket fire. There were many night noises going on around me, and my senses were on full alert.

I was listening and looking. I was also thinking about the last two hours and a lifetime—or so it seemed—of placing myself in harm's way. I was thinking about family, friends, children, America, my soldiers, and asking myself, "Why?" and "Had I done enough?" Also, where was I to go from here? I found most of the answers that night while in lonely thought and contemplation. My wayward journey was coming to a close; I was going home.

It was just another day in Iraq, starting off with early morning mortar engagements on our compound. Then, after the all clear, we had a little late breakfast at the mess hall and then on to another day of visiting, training, and teaching unique people possessing varying skills and from different backgrounds.

It was always different, never routine, and always challenging. I loved my work, and each day was always unique. During that week and on that particular day, we had five US civilian visitors to our compound. It was my task to train and work with them so that they could understand how we did business as well as learn a little something about Iraq. The purpose of my efforts was to assist them in becoming more effective and efficient in helping the Iraqis and the American mission, whatever that was at the time.

My missions have always been open-ended. Both as a special operations soldier and as a senior civilian advisor, my mission statements read something like this: "Go in, see what's up, make something happen." The hidden message in the statement that I was always aware of was, "And don't fuck up, because it's on you if you do," and, of course, "Then get your ass back here."

I have truly been blessed with good mission statements. I think I enjoyed and loved the freedom I had most of my service life. Believe it or not, I built up a pretty good reputation for getting it done and in motivating and training others. It's amazing what a little common sense, a strong work ethic, imagination, enthusiasm, and old country boy ways can do.

One thing a person must have is confidence. Also, don't lose that country flavor. It throws naysayers, enemies, challengers, and the competition off-balance. It definitely worked for me.

That afternoon, after training and the evening meal, the visitors had a helicopter coming in at 2200 hours (10:00 p.m.) to pick them up and get them out of there. As I always did, I walked with them outside the first security compound perimeter to the second-most dangerous perimeter area, the helo pad waiting area and the CONEX bunkers.

That night I didn't take my protective gear. I helped the civilians carry their protective gear and baggage outside the first gate down to the helo pad. My Iraqi terp, Mohamed, also came down that night to help with their gear and to see them off.

During the wait, we occupied ourselves with small talk and goodbyes. It was a positive night so far. The temperature was not too bad. There was a small breeze blowing, and the river could be heard flowing beyond the barbed wire. One of the civilians walked away into the dark, smoking a cigarette. The others, Mo, and I were casually standing around. Everyone had their gear sitting close by, but no one had on their protective gear. I guess one could say we were shooting the breeze, just waiting for the flight to come in.

The first round was a little unusual.

It seemed louder and bigger than the regular nightly reoccurring attack rounds. I found out later that the rockets that night were new ones, much larger and more accurate, and they had been brought in from Iran.

The first rocket hit close but over. The next round went into the tent just over the walkway from us, setting it on fire. I was hoping the kids—the soldiers—got to the bunkers in time. The next round hit really close to the roadway, just outside the CONEX bunker. Mo, my interpreter, was blown about twenty feet from behind a hard concert slab nearby. I had seen him in the blast of light, flying and landing. It looked bad.

While the first three rounds were coming in and hitting, I was busy trying to get my civilians saddled up with their protective gear, vests, helmets, and moved—more like packed—into the CONEX bunker. I was heading back outside to look for the civilian who had disappeared in the dark, when the road blast occurred. As it was coming in, I was diving back through the door of the CONEX. As it hit, my upper body was inside the doorway, where all was quiet and still. By contrast, my lower body and legs were being whipped and slammed violently against the doors by the blast.

This is when I did it. While diving in, I said God's name in vain: "God!" In that short time, as my lower half was violently cast around, and my upper half was inside the doorway, all quiet and safe feeling. I said those words. I was keenly aware of what I had just said as I pulled both of my legs inside and sat up. In that brief moment, I knew something special had just occurred.

I was sitting in a quiet, safe space, and I was whole and free of injury.

I said in a voice raised to heaven, "Forgive me, Lord. I'll never do that again."

Then I quickly gathered myself up, told everyone to stay put, and back I went into the night as the mortar and rockets were continuing to fall but "walking" away from us into the distance. I found Mohammed. He wasn't hurt too badly, as it was the back blast from the explosion that had sent him flying. Then I found the last civilian in another bunker thirty or so yards away, safe.

The soldiers in the tent had made it to a bunker, Mo was okay, and the five civilians were not hurt.

The rockets and mortars came in just as the chopper was coming in to land. They had veered off, but now, as the rounds had fallen off, they had come back in. Then the civilians were quickly picked up, and off they went.

After any attack, all the intel folks and first responders checked out where all the rounds went and how many there were—someone must have been counting them as they came in. Then they put out the fires, located any duds, took care of personnel, and made sure all were accounted for. Once that was taken care of, they gave the all clear, and people went back to their activities.

Most of the time, after an attack, it took a good hour, at least, to account for everything. So, after getting everyone off on the helo and waiting to be able to go back into the safer compound area where my billets were, I had a little time to reflect on life.

Sitting there on top of that sandbag bunker on what had become a clear, still night, watching our return battery about twenty miles away return a fireworks display of hail on enemy positions, I sat there, thinking, *Hell, it's time to go home!*

During my last four years in Iraq, I had two offices hit with mortars or rockets, convoys ambushed, meetings interrupted by small-arms fire, two helos hit, and I was exposed to almost daily mortar firings in the mornings and evenings. I had lost four terps—two killed, one kidnapped, and the other disappeared, never to be heard from again. There were untold bad actors, meetings in hostile places with unfriendly folks, weekly market explosions in nearby towns, wild rides all over Iraq with military and civilian contractors, and impossible tasks with undisciplined, poor, and unskilled foreign actors.

I had fun, but enough was enough. Time to go home. I had a lifetime of stories to tell. I had met along the way an unbelievable array of interesting folks, gained a lifetime of learning, and had experienced life to the fullest. I can't ever remember a dull moment.

I've enjoyed the journey so far and gave it a pretty good "go." I would change only a few things, if I could, but then I would probably mess up if I had the chance. I learned that things happen for a reason. We have to look for that reason and try to make the most of it.

I know my life has been good, and I think I was meant to be an educator with a strong background. I obtained that and hope I can do well in my retirement years with what I have been given. I have been blessed.

Dad always said, "If you love what you do for a living, you'll never work a day."

I've always loved being a soldier, merchant mariner, teacher, electrician, builder, tinker, and a county agent. I really can't remember ever working a day in my life, and I have truly been blessed.

Printed in the United States
by Baker & Taylor Publisher Services